Jonathan Goodman has been described as 'the greatest living master of the true-crime literature' (Jacques Barzun) and 'the premier investigator of crime past' (Julian Symons). Once a theatre director and television producer, he then became managing director of a specialised publishing company. In 1970, his first book, *The Killing of Julia Wallace*, was published and since then, as a full-time writer on crime, he has published nineteen true-crime accounts and four novels. He is one of the few lay-members of the British Academy of Forensic Sciences, a member of the Medico-Legal Society, and is on the committee of the Crime Club. He lives in London.

Also by Jonathan Goodman

Non-fiction

The Killing of Julia Wallace
The Burning of Evelyn Foster
The Stabbing of George Harry Storrs
Bloody Versicles: the Rhymes of Crime
Post-Mortem: the Correspondence of Murder
The Trial of Ian Brady and Myra Hindley
The Trial of Ruth Ellis (with Patrick Pringle)
The Pleasures of Murder (editor)
The Railway Murders (editor)
The Seaside Murders (editor)
The Master Eccentric
The Journals of Rayner Heppenstall, 1969–1981 (editor)
The Crippen File
Who He? Goodman's Dictionary of the Unknown Famous
Underworld (with Ian Will)
Acts of Murder
The Christmas Murders (editor)
The Oscar Wilde File
The Slaying of Joseph Bowne Elwell

Fiction

Instead of Murder
Criminal Tendencies
Hello Cruel World Goodbye
The Last Sentence

Verse

Matinée Idylls

MURDER
in
High Places

JONATHAN GOODMAN

Headline

ISBN 0–7472–3005–6

Headline Book Publishing PLC
Headline House
79 Great Titchfield Street
London W1P 7FN

Printed and bound in Great Britain by
William Collins Sons & Co Ltd,
Glasgow G4 0NB

Contents

List of Illustrations

For K
(Mrs Robert F. Hussey)
With love

Introduction

F. SCOTT FITZGERALD: *The rich are different from us.*
ERNEST HEMINGWAY: *Yes, they have more money.*

I confess responsibility for all of this book apart from its title, which, according to the majority verdict of friends in the world of publishing who claim to be able to tell an unseemly title from one that has what blessedly few of them term pizzazz, is preferable to what I had in mind: 'A Wealth of Murder'. Posing as a democrat, I straightway succumbed to *Murder in High Places* – though I wondered at the time, and do still, whether calling the book that might deceive some people into supposing that it contained tales of hilltop crime: John Watson Laurie's bludgeoning of Edwin Rose on Goatfell, for instance. A greater worry was, and is, that the vicarious entitlers' idea of social High Places didn't much resemble mine.

Presumably, such High Places are inhabited (some might say infested) by members of High Society. But who, or what, are *they*? Have they simply paid for admittance? If so, then many of them are of what Noël Coward described as Nescafé Society. Have the pictures in their passports been cut from *The Tatler*? If so, then there must be a Higher Society, of excessively grand personages who would no more invite a scribbling or snapping Tatler to their gatherings than they would deign to reply to a mid-winter invitation saying Tarzan and Jane Costumes Will Be Worn.

As I have intimated, the subject of wealth is the connector of my criminal tales. Contrary to the impression given by crime novelists, few murders premeditated for longer than an hour or so are motivated by an irresistible desire for financial improvement: wealthy testators rarely expire as a direct result of impatience on the part of their neediest or greediest heirs. And so – and for other reasons – the victims, suspects and culprits referred to in this book are not common. It may be a coincidence of my selection of cases, but I do seem to have lent support to those who complain that

1

there is one criminal law for the middle classes (not the ostensibly poor, whose advisers can be spendthrift with Legal Aid funds), and another for the rich.

My thanks go to friends who have helped in diverse ways – Peter Cotes, Joe Gaute, Robin Odell and Richard Whittington-Egan.

Jonathan Goodman

The Passing
on the Fourth Floor Back

Were you born of some queer magic,
    In your shimmering gown?
Is there something strange and tragic,
    Deep, deep down?

Lines from a lyric by NOËL COWARD

I start uncertainly. I believe that the fusillation of Prince Ali Kamel Fahmy Bey was the first murder case I heard of, but I may be wrong. Perhaps earlier tellings of other murders had gone in one twice-daily-washed ear and out the other. My parents were unconventional bedtime tale-tellers: they referred to, but never actually told me, fairy stories, assuming that I would prefer to hear how Dorothy Ward, boyish as Jack, had scaled a beanstalk and, disappearing from the audience's view, received rapturous applause for her vertical exit; of the Australian Oscar Asche, Chinese as Chu-Chin-Chow; of José Collins, the Maid of the Mountains; of Phyllis Neilson-Terry, Oberon at the Open Air Theatre in Regent's Park. My parents as you will have gathered, were great ones for the theatre. And, for them, 'theatre' was not confined to the stage. And they were what would now be called, I suppose, lateral thinkers: memories were corroborated by other memories, or were jogged into being mentioned by recollection of things that had happened at the time, or in the locality, of things that had stayed, higgledy-piggledy, in their minds.

I know the day of the month when I first heard of the Fahmy case: the seventeenth day of a January between King Edward's announcement on the wireless that he had abdicated (I was too young to be awake for it) and Neville Chamberlain's announcement on what people were starting to call the radio that Great Britain was at war with Germany (I heard that in the cottage at Castle Combe to which, presciently, I had been evacuated). On that 17 January, a birthday for me, my aunts Amy, Henrietta and Rachel were supposed to call; for days before, my mother had hinted that if I behaved myself, the aunts would bear gifts. But – and this could probably fix the year – by the time the table was laid, cake and all, it had started to rain, to pour. The hour arranged for the aunts' arrival passed; my father returned, dripping wet, from work; we were not on the phone, and so the aunts – who had told my mother that they would collect together in Putney and travel *en masse* to Wimbledon – could not explain to us the reason for their absence. I was told, first, to stop making faces, and then to sit at the table, to sit up straight, to eat my allotment of the birthday feast, sticking to the established order of fishpaste sandwich, scone with raspberry preserve, a helping of pink junket, and, if I really wanted it, a slice of cake (which, my memory says, had not been decked with candles for me to blow out). When for the umpteenth time I swallowed (my parents were stern against my speaking with my mouth full) and asked about the aunts, my mother at last spoke critically of them, saying: 'They're frightened of a spot of rain – think they're made of sugar.' However, my father stuck up for them. If what was teeming down outside was a spot, he said, then the Sahara was a sand-castle. He couldn't remember a worse deluge than this – always excepting, of course, that dreadful storm during a summer night in 1923. Very young then, he had been told by much older people that they couldn't remember a worse storm: thunder and lightning as well as the pelting rain. It was the night, he went on, of that shooting at the Savoy Hotel . . . Madame Fahmy, she killed her husband, he as rich as Croesus: a blackguard, peculiar in his appetite for –

Then my mother interrupted, pointing out that such tales were not nice at any time, least of all at the tea-table.

I was grown up before I read about Prince and Madame Fahmy: not so grown up that I did not worry that my mother, by then dead, might have disapproved of my reading about them. Ever since I had worked out that my father had made up a legend on the spur of the moment when, walking me on Wimbledon Common, he had declared that particular hoofprints on the bridle-path near the Leg-o'-Mutton Pond were those of Black Bess, implanted during Dick Turpin's ride to York, I had tended to suspect fabrication of or exaggeration in his tales. But it turned out that he had not overstated the natural violence of the night of the shooting at the Savoy. On 10 July 1923, the *Daily Telegraph* reported that, from round about midnight, London had experienced its worst storm for many years:

> The outbreak appeared to travel from the direction of Kingston and Richmond. Soon afterwards the storm reached London itself, and broke with all its fury at a time when, luckily, most of the theatre-goers had been able to reach their homes in safety. The lightning was vivid to a degree. For over two hours the sky was illuminated by brilliant, continuous flashes that gave the buildings an eerie appearance, and at least once what seemed to be a gigantic fireball broke into a million fragments of dazzling fiery sparks. Equally dramatic were the heavy crashes of thunder which grew in a mighty *crescendo*, intense and majestic, and then into a *diminuendo* as the storm swept irresistibly over the city. The storm followed a day of almost tropical heat.

In the early 1970s I was, between times, general editor of a series of volumes called *Celebrated Trials*. Because of its outcome, the trial of Madame Fahmy had not been reported as a Hodge *Notable British Trial* – nor, inexplicably, had it figured among Geoffrey Bles's inferior *Famous Trials*. Since it could scarcely have been more celebrated, I determined to include it in my series; and as Rayner Heppenstall, among too many avocations a crime historian and a studier of the French people and their language, seemed cut out to edit and introduce the transcript, I invited him to do so. His explanation of why, having accepted the invitation, he, like my aunts, disappointed me is given in the journals he wrote between 1969 and 1981, when he died, and which I edited into a book called *The Master Eccentric*. I have once or twice wondered how he would have told the story of Madame Fahmy. Much as his account of why he didn't differs from the one in my mind, it would have come out merely saliently similar to my version of the events.

I have quoted a description of the storm that was raging as Madame Fahmy fired three bullets into her husband. Now let me quote from *Bella Donna*, a novel by Robert Hichens, published in 1909, and so widely read thereafter that Madame Fahmy's defender at her trial was confident that, in speaking of it, he was striking a chord in the minds of the two women on the jury; of most of the men as well.

> 'Al-làh!' he murmured, saying the word like an Egyptian man.
> He looked into her eyes.

'The first word you hear in the night from Egypt, Ruby; Egypt's night greeting to you. I have heard that song up the river in Nubia often, but – oh, it's so different now!'

During her long experience in a life that had been complex and full of changes, she had heard the sound of love many times in the voices of men, but she had never heard till this moment Nigel's full sound of love. There was something in it that she did not know how to reply to, though she had the instinct of the great courtezan to make the full and perfect reply to the desires of the man with whom she had schemed to ally herself. . . .

He drew a little nearer to her, and she understood, and could reply to the demand which prompted that movement.

'We must drink Nile water together, Ruby – Nile water – in all the different ways. I'll take you to the tombs of the Kings, and to the Colossi when the sun is setting. And when the moon comes we'll go to Karnak. I believe you'll love it all as I do. One can never tell, of course, for another. But – but do you think you'll love it all with me?'

Mingled with the ardour and the desire there was a hint in his voice of anxiety, of the self-doubt which in certain types of natures is the accompaniment of love.

'I know I shall love it all – with you,' she said. . . .

'Ruby!' he exclaimed.

He tried to seize her hand, but she would not let him.

'No, Nigel! Don't touch me now. I – I shall hate you if you touch me now. . . .' She turned hurriedly away.

'Ruby!' he said, with a passion of tenderness.

'No, no! Leave me alone for a little. I tell you I must be alone!' she exclaimed as he followed her.

He stopped on the garden path and watched her go into the house.

'Beast, brute that I am!' he said to himself.

Steamy stuff. But only literally more so than Madame Fahmy's life under that name. Her descriptions of that life – or descriptions of it given by others on her behalf, to the jury by her counsel, to readers of newspapers by reporters, ghost-writers and sob-sisters – erred from reality in particulars but were as accurate as most general truths ever are. Speaking both geographically and culturally, it was a far cry, that Moslem married life of hers, from her earlier existences: farthest of all from the earliest.

She was born to a couple called Alibert, living in a sombre suburb of Paris, on 9 December 1890. Then, perhaps, or earlier or later, her father was a cab-driver. She was given the names of Marie and Marguerite; when she considered herself mature, she sometimes hyphenated the names, sometimes used the second of them only, and was known to friends as Maggie. The names, presumably chosen on an alliterative ground, happened to be the respective true and posthumously-fictive names of the Lady of the Camellias. That comment will become relevant. To save confusion till she can be called Madame Fahmy, I shall refer to her as Marguerite.

Her parents being devout Roman Catholics, she was sent to a convent school: run by Sisters of St. Mary, it was in the Avenue des Ternes, within walking distance of her home. More than a quarter of a century later, she would explain, or agree with the explanation, that *I was very devout myself, in a mystic way, as young, sensitive girls often are.*

None of her kin was well off, but she had a godmother who was very rich indeed. This was Madame Langlois, the wife of one of the several lawyers who, when Marguerite was twelve, assisted Thérèse Humbert, perhaps the most excessive and successful swindler of all time, in squeezing away from a just punishment.[1] *My godmother had very refined tastes, and loved the arts and music. As I lived with her a great deal, my natural leaning towards art was accentuated. I love singing, my voice having been cultivated at the convent, where I sang sacred solos. My voice is mezzo-soprano, and among my favourite pieces is 'Butterfly'. I was an admirer of Mlle. Chenal, an opera star in Paris, and amused myself learning all her parts. In this people said that I succeeded very well.*

Her vocal precocity was – in those days – less remarkable than her sexual forwardness. Soon after her sixteenth birthday, she gave birth to a child, a girl she called Raymonde. The surmise of earlier writers that the father of Raymonde was a Raymond gives Marguerite the benefit of the doubt that she became fecund from her inaugural liaison. So far as I can tell, if the name she gave the child was a clue to the father's identity, she let slip no others. Having suckled Raymonde, Marguerite gave her into the care of an aunt. Within a short time – no more than a couple of months – she became engaged to André Meller, a man of twenty-eight who was better known for being a brother of an owner of racing stables and some horses therein than for any attribute or achievement. *Unfor-*

---

[1] The best account of the case for non-accountants is by Rayner Heppenstall, in *A Little Pattern of French Crime* (London, 1969).

tunately I had not a sufficient dowry, and that first beautiful dream collapsed. We were separated.

I was as tall as I am today, rather stronger, and I had chestnut-red hair falling to my knees. My nature was mercurial, and under my love-sorrow my life quite changed. I left my dear godmother and my family in order to go to friends at Bordeaux with my young sister, who was eight years old at the time. (She gives no hint of how her parents reacted to her sister's departure, let alone her own. It seems sensible to sacrifice chronology to tidiness, and mention here that one of her brothers was killed in an accident, the other while serving on the front near Rheims during the Great War. There must have been times when the Aliberts wished they had stayed childless.) *At Bordeaux, I made the acquaintance of a charming man who loved me deeply. Twice he told me I must be his wife. But always my first deception in love prevented realisation of a definite arrangement of life.* (Is she speaking of the affair that begot Raymonde or of the engagement that was broken for want of a sufficient dowry? One cannot tell.)

The years (about six) *passed. I came back to live in Paris in 1913. I took a flat alone in the rue Pergolese. I led a very quiet and wise life, scarcely going out at all. My daughter was in the country. I expected to be able to smooth away the difficulties which prevented my wedding, and in April, 1913, my marriage was publicly announced. However, Monsieur X (Paul Channon), of Bordeaux, was waiting for the annulment of his first marriage, which was pending at Rome. At the last moment he was not able to obtain satisfaction, and all intention of marriage between us was given up in August, 1913, at Deauville, where I had a villa, and entertained a great many acquaintances. With a view to my marriage we had acquired a magnificent flat in Paris, which I retained on my return from Deauville.*

While in Paris I entertained a great deal. There came to my house a number of actresses, a few celebrities – a very Parisian circle. During the war I served with the Red Cross, driving my own Renault, and sang at charity concerts.

I fell ill and had to enter a nursing home for an operation. A strange romance followed. In the same building, I learned, was an old friend (Charles Laurent), who had come in for the same purpose. During our convalescence we fell in love and were married in 1919.

Laurent's love for her, hers for him, soon proved susceptible to impediment. He was a rare sort of Frenchman in that he was a fluent speaker and artistic writer of Japanese. His facility with that language seems to have caused a longing in him to live where it was native, and when the chance to do so arose, he told Marguerite that he intended to take it, giving up his job as an interpreter at the Japanese Consulate in Paris, and, of course, expected her to migrate with him. The expectation was forlorn. Citing her patriotic deeds during the war – as a transporter of the lame, as a stage-entertainer of the fit (her busyness at each of which she preferred not to boast about) – she told her husband that she would need a far, far better reason for leaving France than going to Japan: unlike him, she was linguistically inept, and the very thought of living in a country so inscrutably foreign appalled her. And so Laurent shrugged Gallicly or bobbed orientally, said that he would help her to effect a divorce (an action which she, despite her Catholicism, was prepared to take), gave her the deeds of his house (which meant that, what with the villa at Deauville and the Paris property conceded to her by the matrimonially encumbered Paul Channon, she was pretty well off for real estate), promised a handsome allowance till such time as she remarried, threw in his motor-car (no common Renault, that), and, saying sayonara, walked out of her life.

Marguerite went on the town; became a talk of it. She gave lavish parties, and – usually with a male escort, rarely the same one twice – attended parties given by others of the Smart Set; on most partyless nights, she whiled the time away in exclusive restaurants and expensive night-clubs, often dancing till the small hours at the latter: *I love dancing, but I do not care for such eccentric dances as the Shimmy. Indeed, I prefer to dance in the English fashion, which I find very correct.* Not all of the daylight hours were spent in bed or preparing for nocturnal fun – buying clothes, having things done to her hair, her fingernails trimmed and lacquered, her face and neck smoothed: sometimes when the weather was fine, she rode or played lawn-tennis or golf, and sometimes when it wasn't, she drove – not to get somewhere but because she enjoyed driving. Once or twice she visited or was visited by her daughter Raymonde, who was at boarding school – and who, she believed (perhaps rightly; I have not enquired into French law on the subject), had been legitimised by her marriage to Charles Laurent.

In January 1922, she and some friends, seeking the sun in an exotic setting, visited Egypt, and – she usually driving the hired limousine, her face shaded by a Paris milliner's version of the sola-topi – toured northern parts of that land, using as their base

Shepheard's in Cairo, which was said by English guests wishing to be complimentary to it to be more English than any English hotel.

On an evening towards the end of their visit, they attended a reception given by an Egyptian acquaintance of one of them. The host was approached by a native guest, who, indicating Marguerite, said: 'Tell her that I will arrange a *fête Vénitienne* on my yacht in her honour.' The host did as he was told, explaining to Marguerite that the offer came from Prince Ali Kamel Fahmy Bey. Before saying yes or no, or murmuring an option-retaining *peut-être*, she asked for information about him.

Fahmy was a playboy of the eastern world. Though only mid-way through his twenty-first year (which meant that he was almost ten years younger than Marguerite), he was among the wealthiest of Egyptians; and, despite his excesses, there seemed no reason why he should not grow richer still – become a millionaire, not just of his own country's pound but in terms of the Bank of England's, too. Keeping to the latter currency, estimates of his annual income ranged from £40,000 to five times that amount. (Multiplying by 14 gives an idea of the purchasing power of such sums today.) He owed his wealth to the death of his father, an engineer by training but a tycoon by vocation, who had bequeathed him the lion's share of his estate: vast cotton plantations throughout northern Egypt, commercial and residential property in and around Cairo, interests in financial institutions, shares in mighty trading companies.

Young Fahmy's education had not been entrusted to Egyptian teachers but to French and English ones, each in their own land – at a well-regarded academy near Paris and at a public school other than Eton or Harrow. At those places he had picked up the respective native languages; had received the tuition in the 'arts of cosmopolitanism' that was stressed in the brochures of those places, setting them apart from less expensive educational establishments. Perhaps partly because in the English school, fellow-students, pink-complexioned whereas he was swarthy, had looked down on him on account of his nationality, he had grown towards manhood cosmopolitan in one sense, determinedly Egyptian in another. Perhaps partly because of his acceptance that he could not disguise his nationality, as soon as he was enriched by his father's will he became intensely nationalistic; and, while often behaving irreligiously, boasted of entire adherence to Mohammedanism. His good works in aid of his country, his countrymen –

grants to clever young Egyptians so that they could study else-where; contributions towards the building of hospitals – seemed munificent to people of modest means, and caused the many who were poor to revere him. When he was already entitled Bey, the head of the government, keen to encourage his charity, said that before long he would receive a higher honour, and that, mean-while, it was perfectly all right for him to call himself a prince; thus he became – oddly, it seems to an Englishman, used to one title supplanting a lesser one – *Prince* Ali Kamel Fahmy *Bey*.

Most of his friends called him Ali; some of the others, few of them Egyptian, referred to him, even to his face, as Baba – a nickname less likely to have been derived directly from the tale of the Forty Thieves, told on one of the Thousand and One Nights, than from the Chu-Chin-Chowing of it that had been performed on 2238 nights or afternoons at His Majesty's Theatre in London's Haymarket, for the last time only months before. Ali, a frequent visitor to London, had seen the show several times, always from the same stage-side box, and may have been provoked by it into presenting, for one night only in a grand Mayfair house, a truly Arabian spectacular – that being (if the sole critic to write of it got things straight) 'a Terpsichorean celebration, carried out with many mystic accompaniments, of the Goddess of the Sun, Ta Aha'. Ali took no performing part in the presentation; but it seems that he might undisgracingly, have done, had he felt like exchang-ing his Saville Row suit for raiment resembling that worn by Egyptians of thirty-five centuries before. Ballroom dancing was one of Ali's favourite public pastimes: gossip-columnists of Cairo's papers, ordered by their editors to publicise the Prince (but not to speak of certain of His unmusical amusements) spun yards of admiring print, all of it devoted to His excellence and endurance as two-stepper and tangoist, repeating – over and over again but ever with a tone of wonder – words like 'twinkling', 'lithe' and 'sinuous' with regard to His mastery of motion in time with the New Music from America and Europe.

Having been told at least some of all of this, and maybe other things, by her host, relayer of Ali's offer of a *fête*, Marguerite repaired to a powder-room, where she smoked a Regie as an aid to deciding how to respond. Her mind made up, she emerged, and when her host enquired what message he should take to the Prince, told him: '*Non, merci.*' (*Naturally I felt intrigued at the thought of such a personality, but somehow or other I felt that it was better to refuse.*)

It seems unlikely that she was being subtle; playing hard-to-get. The fact that she was returning to Paris in a day or so would surely have erased the thought, if the thought has entered her head, of playing that game in which a man chases a woman to where she means to catch him. Absence, so long as it is not prolonged, may, just may, make the heart of an established lover grow fonder; but the absence of someone who has simply aroused interest at first sight is almost bound to diminish the interest till, soon, the interesting party is barely recollectable, never intentionally thought of.

Therefore, however conceited she was, Marguerite must have been surprised when, a few months later, towards the end of springtime in Paris, she saw a now-fezless Ali peering at her across a crowded room. He did not approach her; she pretended that she had not noticed him. At subsequent swell-elegant gatherings, he peered at her from the outskirts, and she, centre-stage, feigned unawareness of his gaze. Now she *was* playing hard-to-get. And she played at that harder still when, following more non-encounters, Ali sought an introduction. She declined to meet him.

By now, it was July. She spent part of that month at Deauville, and there got to know a woman from Morocco. Or rather (and the reason for saying this will soon be apparent), was befriended by the woman. When she mentioned that she was returning to Paris, the woman said that she was going there too, and begged a lift. During the drive, the woman chattered about her past with such indiscretion that Marguerite felt that it would be impolite not to return the compliment.

A day or so later, the woman telephoned Marguerite, saying: 'I have a friend who absolutely must make your acquaintance. He says that it is his sole ambition while he is in Paris.'

Mystified, I agreed to a rendezvous for tea in the lounge of the Majestic Hotel on the 30th. When I walked into the lounge and again found fixed upon me the large, dark eyes of the man whom I knew to be Ali Fahmy, I experienced a curious tressaillement. *The thought had never occurred to me that the individual who so longed to meet me was this Egyptian 'prince'.*

Only the middle one of those sentences can be accepted as almost-whole truth. Were it not for the inclusion of the word 'curious', it would be a model of veracity. There was nothing at all curious about her *tressaillement*. Though she was a practised siren, she would have had to be made of stone not to be thrilled.

Once the introduction had been effected, and the introducer had departed (and was now, presumably, Morocco-bound, having completed her assignment), Ali set about sweeping Marguerite off her dainty feet.

He suggested going to the Château de Madrid, and I agreed. As we walked to the door there came the first incident revealing how he sought always to carry out an affair en prince. Pointing to two superb cars, one a Rolls-Royce coupé limousine and the other a dazzling 'torpedo', he said: 'Which do you prefer?' With, I am afraid, rather an amused smile, I said I would prefer the closed car.

Let me describe, if I can, Ali's appearance. He was a man of exceptional powers of fascination. He would be about five feet nine inches in height, and though he did not go in for athletics, he was of singularly muscular and powerful build. Never have I met a man who possessed to such a degree that kind of charm which we are accustomed to call Oriental. About his black hair there was just a reddish tint – most unusual in one of his race. His eyes were remarkably expressive, striking one with the exceptionally caressing quality of their glance, but suddenly hardening on occasions into a ferocity which was positively terrifying.

Most of the conversation during our first meeting consisted of gentle raillery concerning my having avoided him for so long.

Both made up for the lost time. Towards the end of the return journey from the Château de Madrid, Marguerite agreed to be driven somewhere almost as splendid the next day; this despite the fact that Ali's vanity was exemplified by his driving, which brooked no interference from lesser road-users; he was, she decided, straightway telling him so, a 'velocimaniac'. During the following fortnight, there were more car-trips; together, they joined in galas; near the end of the period, they enjoyed each other's company tête-a-tête, both at her residence and in his suite at the Majestic; she introduced him to her friends, and he displayed her to his. And she got to know, or had pointed out to her, the members of his entourage: foremost, Said Enani, whose responsibilities were greater and more varied than those of most private secretaries; also a lawyer, a second secretary, a black valet, and a bodyguard-cum-chauffeur – later referred to by Marguerite as a 'chocolate-coloured Colossus'.

In mid-August, she returned to Deauville, accompanied by a girl-friend. And Ali went there, too. *At Deauville a more serious note began to creep into his expressions of affection. Then rapidly he made* des avances furieuses. *But I would not yield, and after three days of vain supplication he decided to leave and go to Italy. Fervently he tried to persuade my friend and myself to travel with him. He besought, implored, entreated; but I would not listen. At last, with a great show of temper, he flung himself off. Whether by his instructions or not, I do not know, but before the departure Said Enani began to boast to me of Ali's great fortune and the wonderfully luxurious life he led in his palace at Cairo. At this stage there were only thrown open gates through which with the eyes of imagination I could dimly perceive some of the splendours which awaited his wife.*

Of the following sentence a cynic might remark: If you believe this, you'll believe anything.

What, however, appealed to me most about Ali was his smile, which was like that of a child.

Yet behind it was that well-developed jaw, which, as I experienced before long, could set any moment into cruel outline.

But at present all was charm and sweetness. As I was going to Biarritz on the first of September, I promised to allow him to accompany me. For eight days in that wonderful resort he was so affectionate that I felt my whole being suffused with a sort of radiant sympathy towards him. These were perhaps the happiest days of my life. We made excursions to San Sebastian in Spain, St. Jean de Luz, where we dined in 'La Réservée', decorated like a miniature fairyland. He was always accompanied by the same train of attendants. Money was poured out lavishly. Nothing was too good, too beautiful, or too dear for me. Cartier's was ransacked for the latest creation in jewellery, and Ali chose and gave me a really beautiful bracelet of coral and emeralds.

Still Ali wanted to take her to Italy; still she refused. Even when he said, 'I will marry you. Come,' she said no. And so he went to Milan alone – except, of course, for his half-dozen minions. *From there commenced a series of wonderful letters couched in the extravagant phraseology of the Orient. When, at the end of September, he went to Egypt, he wrote that he was sick with despair, and that I must come. He sent me tickets for the journey, but I replied that I would not go until later. Then he started to bombard me with telegrams, using every artifice to get me to go to Egypt immediately. 'I am dying,' he said. 'Your name alone is on my lips.' I could resist no longer and said I would travel on 17 November.*

Concerned that she might change her mind – perhaps because of hearing tittle-tattle about him – Ali wrote more letters. One began, 'My dear little Bella,' and read, in part:

Your presence everywhere pursues me incessantly. These are not memories I am invoking, they are realities. Sincerity – it is so difficult to find. Confidence and sincerity, cause and effect. I believe I have obtained it and I believe I have merited it. I believe I have proved sufficiently that I am worthy of it. How can one fail to recognise qualities which stand out so blindingly clear?

Torch of my life – you appear to me surrounded by a halo. I see your head encircled by a crown which I reserve for it here. It is a crown I have reserved for you on your arrival in this beautiful country of my ancestors. If you abandon your journey scheme, you will have made my life aimless. Envy and jealousy should never have any weight with any of us. Come, come quickly, and appreciate the beautiful sun of Egypt. My only consolation is you. Believe me, I love you very much. From your faithful Little Baba.

Marguerite's contribution to the correspondence was comparatively slight; and her notes tended to deal with practical matters. For instance, she asked about the arrangements for her accommodation in Cairo.

His reply was a magnificent gesture. 'You shall have my palace', he declared splendidly. 'As for me, I will live in my Daira' (a word meaning, in effect, his offices).

(Actually, the gesture was not all that magnificent. Ali's offices, in the centre of Cairo, were sumptuous; part of a mansion set in acres of garden, and with stables and garages at the rear.)

She reached Alexandria on 22 November. *There was Ali, armed with special permission, coming on board to seek me out. A powerful motor-car was waiting, and in this we swiftly travelled to his villa, a few miles from Alexandria on the sea-coast – the Biarritz of Egypt. The journey to Cairo was made by train, where we arrived three hours later. Making our way through a crowd of Arabs, we stepped into a powerful car, drove through the town, and reached the palace of Zamalik on the other side of the Nile. Two other cars followed with the luggage and the servants.*

I was installed like a princess. Twelve black servants in uniforms laced with gold awaited us at intervals on the steps. The interior of the palace is a copy of Fontainebleau – wonderful marble, splendid tapestries, furniture of Aubusson Louis XVI, old Persian carpets, and there is Empire plate, delicately chased, worth 550,000 francs.

My own room had been designed for the King of Serbia and on his instructions before that dreadful year 1914. On the wall are marvellous blue and gold silk hangings. The bed rests on a huge dais in the shape of a boat. Around it are carven bronze figures. A canopy in the same silk as that which covers the walls, draped with real lace and surmounted by immense white ostrich plumes, rises dome-like above the bed. There are two secretaires, a Psyche glass with huge columns, a white and gold couch with a little white and gold table, all in the Empire style. On the dressing-table is a complete toilet set in gold and tortoiseshell. The bathroom is like a Greek temple, in white marble. An arch in the same rich stone rises canopy-like over the centre, enshrining, as it were, a massive solid silver bath. Between the marble columns on either side are draperies of real lace. Between them stand toilette tables of carved onyx and a divan covered with gold lace.

On the smaller household requisites for personal use Ali had spent a small fortune. There were, for example, so many solid gold cigarette boxes that they got in the way.

Ali had had my monogram in diamonds worked on all my objets de toilette. It was almost impossible to find any convenient article in the living rooms on to which he had not somehow or other contrived to introduce what he called his family crest; this, of course, he had designed himself. It was composed of a fantastic reproduction in Arabic of his own name. This strange-looking device was on the uniform of all the servants in appropriate material or gold lace. Where possible, it was picked out in precious stones.

While my eyes were still dazzled, Ali told me that he had prepared all this for me. (It was natural, his saying that he had made the preparations; but, in fact, he had simply paid for what Said Enani had decided to lay on. Ali had given his so-called secretary an incentive to be excessive, this being the perk of a payment of five per cent of the entire bill; since, it is reasonable to assume, Said Enani received commission from most of the dealers and decorators, he was considerably enriched through his master's desire to impress Marguerite into marriage.)

'You are to become my wife,' Ali went on. 'You are my only happiness.' I refused, saying, 'Later, later. Let me become accustomed to the idea.'

I had, indeed, reason to reflect. Already I was realising the difference between the modes of life of East and West.

Having reflected, Marguerite succumbed.

Ali hired a banqueting room at Shepheard's for a celebratory feast, an engagement party writ large, at which the guests – potentates, captains of industry, members of the diplomatic corps, the wives or concubines of some of all of these, playboy friends of Ali, his relatives (most of whom were on his payroll, one aunt for

the unprincely sum of a pound a week) – were stupefied by count-
less courses, as geographically diverse as red caviare, soufflé Suis-
sesse, and skewered chunks of Scotch beef and Jerusalem artichoke.

Thankfully, it seems to me, the marriage ceremonies were, if not
simple, unblatant; the only people to profit from them were civil
servants, priests, and attorneys. There was not even musical
accompaniment. The civil contract was made on 26 December.
Ignoring the protests of a representative of her inherited religion,
Marguerite agreed to declare, '*La ilah illa Lah wa Mohamad Rassoul
Alluh*' (which means, so I have been told, 'There is one God, and
Mohammed is His Prophet'), thus becoming a Moslem, like Ali;
and, again acceding to a wish of his, honoured his mother by
signing the documents in that woman's name of Munira, which
means 'shining'. Then, with Marguerite dressed in black and
having to be led because of the near-opaqueness of a heavy black
veil, a religious ceremony got under way at Ali's Daira. All went
well till, coming as a complete surprise to her, she was asked to
waive the right of divorce. It seems that she had attended a
Moslem version of a confirmation class, for she knew, at least, that
Moslem husbands had plenty of licence: their wives – unless they
had, premaritally, been wary, and stubborn in sticking up for their
rights – virtually none. Salient now was her knowledge that Ali
could cast her aside simply by getting a couple of witnesses to say
that he had remarked, 'I put away this woman'; or, wanting variety
while wishing to retain her, could take on as many as three more
wives and yet be matrimonially lawful. And so she jibbed at the
thought of being bound to Ali, like it or not, till death did them
part. There was an adjournment to a proximate salon of the prin-
cipals, their respective advisers, and the priests, leaving the
guests, uncomfortable on antique upright chairs and not permitted
to chat, not even to make expeditions to *toilettes*, to gaze at the
deserted stage, pretending continued pleasure in the occasion. For
four solid hours. Though Marguerite never subsequently said so,
the deadlock was broken at last by Ali's offering of a gift, in return
for guaranteed constancy, of such prodigiousness that she just
couldn't refuse. All formalities over, the wedding party, each
person of it by now fatigued, repaired to Shepheard's, where a
banquet made ready hours before was revitalised, served, and
devoured with a hunger uncharacteristic of the hotel's clientele.

During the honeymoon – a cruise on Ali's largest yacht along the

Nile, to and from Luxor – Marguerite was, so she afterwards said, given cause to regret having agreed to the till-death clause. If one believes her assertion that she had not permitted the bachelor Ali to use her body, she was presumably surprised, perhaps even shocked, by the way in which he used it; he had spoken of his responsibility to extend the Fahmy dynasty, but his sexual *modus operandi*, done behind her back, so to speak, was neither purposely nor incidentally towards that end. Being petite of rump, she was physically pained as well as mentally disturbed by his unconventional approach. Anticipation of what was to come gloomed her days; was, chronically, quite as misery-making as the nightly coming. Protest made Ali pout, but also roughened his vigour; excuses or, soon, visible causes for denying him entry were ignored. Marguerite put two and two together – her subjection with recollections of Ali's fondling friendliness towards pretty youths, some of whom augmented their prettiness cosmetically – and came up with the inexact answer that Ali was either quite homosexual or transsexual, and that, whichever he was, the bedtime pleasure he derived from her was wholly or intermittently due to a fantasising that her body was male. The fuzzy understanding upset her: if for no other reason than that, having grown used to being adored, her self-esteem, fragile because she had had no need to bolster it, collapsed when pricked by the realisation that a man – now, officially, the only man in the rest of her life – looked upon her as a sexual surrogate.

As if it were not bad enough that she was demeaned in private, Ali – until the one-sided marriage contract was signed and sealed, obsequious in his ostensible reverence of her – was pleased to degrade her in the eyes of his henchmen and of the crew of and helpers aboard the yacht (well-attended degrading, then, for the vessel had a crew of twenty-five, and carried a *chef de cuisine* and his half-dozen assistants, two stewards, and a maid). On an occasion when she remonstrated with him for abusing a seaman, he shouted at her to the effect that as she so enjoyed the company of sailors, she would no doubt appreciate being left alone with an entire crew; then, calling his entourage to heel, he went ashore, and remained there for some hours. Another time, having decided to go ashore, he forbade Marguerite to leave the yacht. 'Surely,' she said, unwittingly mimicking an ingénue in an Adelphi melodrama, 'you will not imprison me on my own honeymoon?' 'The yacht is beautiful,' he replied, 'and you have many servants. Stay here.' Thinking to ensure her obedience, he made up a guard from four of his employees ('veritable giants . . . black colossi,' they seemed to her; whether they were of the crew or temporary, duration-of-honeymoon members of his entourage, one cannot make out) and, still not satisfied with the security, ordered the gangplank lifted behind him. After a sensible wait, she demanded of the quartet that they stop surrounding her and told one of them to drop the gangplank. Severally and singularly, they obeyed. But she had been lulled into a false sense of achievement. Moving to the opening in the rail, she looked across to the embankment – and saw that four more black colossi were stationed there. (Where they had been mustered from is anyone's guess.)

The town of Luxor had been much in the news since 4 November, when British archeologists had found, not far away, the tomb of King Tutankhamün. Arriving there, the Fahmys jaunted to the Valley of the Kings. While subterranean, Ali, a keen snapper, got Marguerite to lie, eyes closed, fingers laced on her breast, in a sarcophagus that till recently had held the dust of a long-dead king, and, as Said Enani made a flash, captured a likeness of her that must, surely, have been deemed eccentric enough to occupy the centre-spread of the honeymoon album.

The setting for the snap may have put an idea into Ali's mind – or into Marguerite's. A day or so after the honeymoon, while closeted in her bedroom, she wrote a statement; the following September, it would be made an exhibit, translation attached, in an English courtroom, would be headlined as THE SECRET DOCUMENT in newspapers throughout the world.

> I, Marie Marguerite Alibert, of full age, of sound mind and body, formally accuse, in the case of my death, violent or otherwise, Ali Fahmy Bey, of having contributed in my disappearance.
> Yesterday, 21 January 1923, at three o'clock in the afternoon, he took his Bible or Koran – I do not know how it is called – kissed it, put his hand on it, and swore to avenge himself upon me tomorrow, in eight days, a month, or three months, but I must disappear by his hand. This oath was taken without any reason, neither jealousy, bad conduct, nor a scene on my part.
> I desire and demand justice for my daughter and for my family.
> Done at Zamalik, at about eleven o'clock in the morning, 22 January 1923.
>
> M. MARGUERITE ALIBERT

P.S. Today he wanted to take my jewellery from me. I refused; hence a fresh scene.

The statement, folded within a plain envelope (not a crested one, because Ali kept a tally of those), went to her lawyer in Paris.

Soon afterwards, apparently (dates of incidents are scarce in this period of the tale), Ali likewise sent a letter to Paris. Addressed to Marguerite's sister, it read, in part:

The question of my marriage, unfortunately, with Munira: Ha, ha, ha, just now I am engaged in training her. Yesterday, to begin, I did not come in to lunch or to dinner, and I also left her at the theatre. This will teach her, I hope, to respect my wishes. With women one must act with energy to be severe.

It is a small pity that one doesn't know which theatre, or what sort of theatre, figured in Ali's training programme. A place in wherever Cairo's Soho was would have been the ideal choice, for just as Marguerite was fastidious as to how she danced, never venturing to shimmy, her taste in stage entertainment was prim. Unlike Ali's: *He frequented those Arab theatres which are a kind of music-hall and which no self-respecting woman can visit.*

During March and April, Ali the trainer teased his trainee with unmeant promises that if she was good, he would take her to Europe. But early in May, a friend, highly placed in the Egyptian government, advised him to accept a sinecure diplomatic position in Paris, saying that a brief spell as a seeming servant of his country would be noted by its title-bestowers and contract-givers, doing him no harm at all. And so he, with his entourage and Marguerite, set sail from Alexandria. Perhaps because he wanted to give Marguerite a nice surprise, or perhaps not, he kept her guessing about the destination till disembarkation at Marseilles.

A suite for them, rooms for his followers, had been reserved at the Majestic. Fresh among the followers, and looming over those longer employed, was an Algerian; called Le Costaud on account of his looming, and thought of by Marguerite as the 'Black Hercules', he took turns with the chauffeur at guarding Ali (who, having taken to wearing an extravagance of jewellery, was as much at risk of being stolen as of being kidnapped) and the rest of the time kept tags on Marguerite. Ali, liking the idea of being called a diplomat, spent a lot of time pretending to be one, and this meant that Marguerite was almost as free in Paris – though often dogged by Le Costaud – as when it had been her home. She visited friends, went riding (a fact that may seem surprising shortly), attended the opera, listened to concerts. And she consulted a doctor; and then, at the latter's instigation, was examined by a specialist surgeon.

At the start of July, Ali, fagged from more than a month of diplomacy, announced that he was taking a holiday. In London. Marguerite pleaded to be left behind, but he would not hear of it.

She was of the Prince's party that arrived at the Savoy Hotel on Sunday, 1 July. He and she were installed in a suite on the fourth floor – at the rear of the building, away from the noisy Strand (where, said the legend, if one lingered long enough and took not a wink of sleep, one would see, passing by, the entire rest of the white population of the world), and so with a fine view of the Thames, Waterloo Bridge on the left, to the north-east, and Hungerford Bridge farther away (and just as well, for it was rather an eyesore) on the right. The others at once or eventually went to rooms either two storeys below or three above; last of all, Ali's valet and Marguerite's pair of maids.

The longer the party stayed in town, the harder the valet and the maids had to work, for on each succeeding day the sweatiness of the master and his wife required more frequent bathing or dabbing of their bodies, more frequent exchanging of moist garments for dry ones. The increasing workload was chiefly caused by the ever more uncomfortable sultriness of a heatwave that Londoners, lobster-faced, sopping wet, odoriferous, in danger, some of them, from apoplexy, told one another, alluding to the usual miserable weather, that they couldn't complain about – but Ali and Marguerite would not have needed so much renovation had their joint and individual appointment cards been left with a few gaps, breaks from the Gay Social Whirl of the capital.

Sometimes together, sometimes separately, the Fahmys worked hard at being Smart; and Marguerite managed to fit in daily visits from Dr. Edward Gordon, whose surgery, also his residence, was just across the Strand, in Southampton Street. (One gathers that general-practitioner Gordon had come to a mutually-rewarding arrangement with the person in charge of the information desk at the Savoy; that when Marguerite, on the day of her arrival, had asked to be put in touch with a doctor, a phone call from an informer had caused Gordon to change from Sabbath casualwear into his uniform of black jacket, striped trousers, spats, cravat and things, grab his gladstone, and hasten to the hotel.) Marguerite's ailment was that for which she had obtained advice and medication in Paris. Gordon probed and prescribed, and then, after eight daily visits (during some of which the patient's husband was present in the suite, but did not say a word), came on the morning of the following day, Monday the ninth, with a specialist colleague – who, having peered at the problem, advised Marguerite to enter a nursing home, *his* nursing home, without delay, there to receive the benefit of his surgical skills. She accepted a modicum of the advice, saying that she would cancel engagements after that night's.

Shortly before or soon after the doctors' visit, a bell-boy, offered an encouraging tip by someone in the foyer for delivering to Marguerite a tightly-sealed envelope *when she was alone*, carried out the mysterious errand, and scampered back to bag the reward. Inside the envelope was a note in French, unsigned, which read:

> Please permit a friend who has travelled widely among Orientals, and who knows the craftiness of their acts, to give you some advice.
>
> Do not agree to return to Egypt, or even Japan, for any object. Rather abandon fortune than risk your life. Money can always be recovered by a good lawyer; but think of your life. A journey means a possible accident, a poison in the flower, a subtle weapon that is neither seen nor heard. Remain in Paris with those who love you and will protect you.

The coupling of Japan with Egypt may have made Marguerite wonder whether the writer, whoever he or she was, knew of the Orient-obsessed Charles Laurent. And certainly, so she was to say to a lawyer a few days later, the reference to 'a poison in the flower, a subtle weapon that is neither seen nor heard,' jogged her memory of how on more than one occasion she, with others, had drunk coffee in the palace at Zamalik – and straightway afterwards, singularly in the gathering, been taken ill.

But the latter thought did not put her off lunch, taken with Ali and Said Enani in one of the Savoy's eating-places. Towards the end of the meal – irritatingly to ruminative neighbours, entertainingly to others, loving scenes or liking reasons to growl, 'bloody foreigners' – Ali and Marguerite loudly argued. The subject was her proposed operation. Said Enani, taking no part in the squabble, not even as mediator or shusher, afterwards swore that it was sparked off by a *fait-accompli* remark by Marguerite to the effect that she was returning to Paris to have the operation there; that it was exacerbated by her refusal to consider Ali's suggestion that she should enter an English nursing home.

The secretary's version is corroborated by the fact that, some time between the doctors' departure and the lunch, Marguerite had told an hotel employee to make Paris-bound travel arrangements for her. And yet, at some time after the lunch – and before about half-past two, the next morning – she wrote a note to Dr. Gordon:

> Doctor: Affairs have come to a crisis. My husband refuses to take the responsibility for my operation. I am therefore returning to my family – that is to say, tomorrow I leave for Paris. Will you excuse me to the doctor who was kind enough to look at me? Believe me, yours gratefully, M. FAHMY
>
> Will you please pay the doctor for his trouble? This account is a personal one.

Perhaps the sequence of events was: she told Gordon's specialist colleague that she would enter his nursing home; (having mulled over the anonymous note?) she decided to have the operation done in Paris, and spoke to the Savoy's travel arranger; lunch; she wrote the change-of-mind note to Gordon – but neglected to send it.

There seems to be no credible testimony as to how the Fahmys spent the afternoon and early evening of that Monday. However, it is reasonable to surmise that if at times they were together, there were addenda to the lunchtime contretemps – that though both of them, Ali especially, were used to extreme humidity, they were made more snappy by the fact that, as the *Daily Telegraph* put it next morning, Monday was 'a day of almost tropical heat'.

Excepting the lessee of the Open Air Theatre in Regent's Park, London's impresarios hated the heatwave, which was vastly diminishing passing trade at their box-offices. Productions that had not attracted much advance booking were in peril from the weather. The show at Daly's, in Leicester Square, was not one of those. Sixteen years before, Daly's had housed the first London production of a play with music by Franz Lehar; now the play had returned to that theatre, was again successful. *The Merry Widow*, it was called. Soon after the Fahmy party's arrival in town, Ali, keen on Viennese music because he was so adept at dancing to it, had insisted on seeing the show, had insisted that Marguerite and Said

Enani accompany him. A further insistence on getting a box had meant that the night for *The Merry Widow* had to be that of Monday, 9 July.

It is, I think, apposite to recall the joke in the form of a question to the just-widowed Mrs Lincoln: 'Apart from that, how did you enjoy the show?' How Ali or Marguerite or Said Enani enjoyed the show at Daly's doesn't seem to have been revealed – perhaps because, when, shortly thereafter, two of them were plied with questions owing to the absence of the third, theatrical enjoyment was a topic that seemed not merely irrelevant but in doubtful taste to broach. Even more shortly afterwards, when all three were seated at a table in the Savoy Grill, eating and, as will be proved, drinking wine, one of them, Marguerite, turned down a perfect opportunity to indicate that she had enjoyed the night at the theatre and desired a recollection of it. The leader of the band asked her if she would like a particular tune to be played, and was told (in French, you may need to be reminded): 'I don't want any music – my husband has threatened to kill me tonight.' Already backing away, the musician, who must have been bilingual, murmured: 'I hope you will be here tomorrow, madam.' Before or after that exchange, she shouted at Ali: 'Shut up! or I'll smash this' (indicating a bottle of Château Mouton Rothschild) 'over your head.' From those two incidents one can draw the induction that the after-theatre supper was not a gay occasion.

It broke up after midnight. Despite the pelting rain, the thunder and lightning, Ali stalked out to the forecourt and took a cab to somewhere off Piccadilly. (Although the driver was subsequently interviewed by the police, Ali's dropping-off place was never revealed: which raises the suspicion that it was a den of such vice that the authorities fuzzed its exact whereabouts, and said nothing of its amenities, for fear of being accused of drumming up business on behalf of the proprietor – or of raising awkward questions as to why no attempt had been made, or was being made, to close the place.) Said Enani may have accompanied his master; if not, he went to his bedroom on the second floor. Certainly, Marguerite took an elevator to the suite at the back of the fourth floor.

Wherever it was that Ali went, he did not stay there long. He was back at the Savoy, and in the suite, before two o'clock . . .
    . . . and out of the suite, loitering in the oyster-grey-carpeted,

silvery-grey-walled corridor, by about thirty minutes past that hour.

John Beattie, a night-porter who happened to be wheeling a trolleyload of luggage along the corridor, feigned unobservance of the guest, who was – so far as Beattie had made out from one subtle glance – wearing only admittedly buttoned-up and tightly-tasselled pyjamas of mauve silk and backless slippers of green velvet. Beattie continued his wheeling, eyes downcast, swerving to the left a little so that there was no fear of the trolley's well-lubricated castors running over the guest's toes. As he was about to pass, the guest issued an order:

'Look at my face! Look what she has done!'

Beattie paused in his wheeling and, since he had been told to, looked – and saw, but only just, a slight pink mark on the guest's left cheek. The door to one of the rooms of the suite was ajar; the room was lit merely by a table lamp, and while Beattie was doing as he had been told, lightning blazed through the windows and across the room and into the corridor, silhouetting the guest and rimming his pyjamas to a sort of purple.

As if cued by the subsequent rattle of thunder, the other door of the suite was flung open, and a woman – beautiful, Beattie couldn't help but notice – stepped into the corridor. Beattie's first impression – a reasonable one considering the male guest's attire, the wee small hour – was that she was wearing a knobby nightgown. But even before she started shrieking words of French at the man, Beattie understood that the garment was a low-cut, sleeveless evening-dress, fashioned almost entirely from shimmering white beads. Flustered away from subservience, he requested the couple to return to the suite, to stop making a disturbance in the corridor – and then instantly showed that he knew his place by bowing neutrally at the wall between the disputants before going on his way, faster than before.

He had wheeled for ten yards or so when, hearing a whistle and assuming that he was being commanded to take notice, he looked over his shoulder – only to see that the male guest, now solitary, was snapping his fingers at an oblivious small dog, perhaps a puppy, that must have ambled out of the suite. (Had one or both of the Fahmys bought or been given the dog? Seemingly so. I have found no reference to the animal's antecedents, no mention of what became of it – and so I am reminded of the black cat that slipped into the Wallace murder case, supped evidential milk, then disappeared for good.)

A moment after Beattie had turned the corner towards the front of the hotel, there was a loud bang – and almost at once another – and almost at once a third. None to do with the storm.

Deserting the trolley, he hastened back to the corner and looked along the corridor to where his journey had first been interrupted.

A tableau.

The lovely woman was standing stock-still. Her right arm was stretched diagonally down, and, like an obscene mechanical extension of it, a pistol was clutched in her hand. The hem of her shimmering white dress was polka-dotted – not in a blemishing way but quite prettily: much as an impressionist artist of her country would have expressed Poppies in the Snow.

The tidiness of the woman contrasted with the mess her pistol pointed at. A spilled bundle of mauve and green materials, dusky skin, black hair; all splashed, and splashed round about on the oyster-grey carpet, with blood. (Hours later, when the body, straightened and bare, was explored by a pathologist, it was found that, ancillary to the salient fact that death was due to severe laceration of brain tissues, one of the bullets had caused four wounds, another two – suggesting that the victim, just before he fell, had contorted his arms to make an inefficient shield for his torso, his face, and that after he had fallen, even when he was dead, his arms had stayed in the peculiar angles of forlorn protectiveness.)

Beattie ran towards the scene – bravely until, when he was a few steps away, the woman threw the pistol beside the body. He knelt, pocketed the pistol, looked at the man's glistening face and saw that he was not yet dead but soon would be. Meanwhile – and we are dealing only in seconds – the woman was saying, over and over again, 'What have I done?' At least, that is what Beattie thought she said. Did he, knowing some French, translate the question the moment it was asked, or did he afterwards speak his remembrance of the sounds so that someone knowing French could turn them into words? The former possibility is not unlikely. True, he was English and menial, but if he had soldiered in France during the war, he must have picked up and may have retained some knowledge of the language. (My father, illicitly youthful when he volunteered for the Royal Flying Corps, was, within weeks of being enlisted, posted to Mesopotamia; and long after surviving the expedition, he sought to impress me by saying things in what he said was Arabic.)

Accounts of what happened during the next several minutes are confused, confusing; there are gaps, and it is sometimes hard to make out the chronology of events. Beattie must have gone into the suite and used the house-phone to summon other employees; before he did so or by the time he had made the call, the corridor was littered with awakened guests; assisted, forced, or of her own volition, Madame Fahmy, weeping and trembling by now, returned to the suite.

Foremost among the employees who hastened to the fourth floor back were Thomas de Bich, the assistant manager of the Savoy, and Arthur Mariani, a night-manager. Both claimed fluency in French. Mariani, who was as brilliantined and musta-chioed as his name suggests, had been ready clothed, and so was the more prompt. Having noted the untidiness in the corridor, he clapped his hands at Beattie and told him to squeeze a pillow under the head and to lay a sheet over the remainder – taking care, he added (for, trained to observe minutiae, he had seen tiny bubbles of reddened spittle drooling from the mouth, perhaps a sign of life), not to cover the face. He may also have issued other orders to other employees: for instance, to persuade guests back to their rooms, to accelerate the progress of medical men, to alert the Savoy's PR and press officers to a need for diminishment of harmful publicity, and, once such vital tasks had been accomplished, to telephone a high-ranking Metropolitan Policeman, out-lining what had occurred and requesting that the detectives assigned to look into it be reasonably spruce and nicely-spoken.

Mariani's recollection of his interview with Madame Fahmy was, so he said, uncertain – 'because it took place in the awful storm, during the flash of the lightning and the crash of the thunder'. She was 'agitated and excited. She said in French, "What have I done? What will happen?" I asked why she had done this, and she replied, "I have been married six months, and I have suffered terribly." I also understood her to say that she and her husband had quarrelled about divorce.'

Thomas de Bich (whose surname, I have been told, was amend-ed to a behind-his-back sobriquet by his British subordinates) found Madame Fahmy 'very frightened and distressed. She caught hold of my arm and then all of a sudden dropped down dazed.' When recovered, she asked the same question of De Bich as she had asked of Mariani (or maybe they both heard a once-asked question): 'What have I done?' She also said something that De Bich at the time translated as 'I have lost my head' but which afterwards, helpfully to her, he admitted might have been 'I was frightened out of my wits'.

Did Mariani and De Bich leave her alone in the suite? It seems that they did, since neither of them subsequently said anything about a call that she made on the house-phone to Said Enani. The ringing woke him at about 2.40, he reckoned. Her voice was crackling through the receiver before he had it to his ear. He muttered a sleepy something, then was instantly made wide-awake by *'Venez vite, venez vite! J'ai tiré sur Ali!'* – which was one of the few of her utterances shortly after the shooting which would be translated for her prosecutors uncontroversially so far as her pro-tectors were concerned: there would be no attempt to tamper with 'Come quickly, come quickly! I have shot at Ali!'

Said Enani – 'in a very bad state of nerves' – went quickly to the fourth floor back, but arrived only just in time to see his master being carried on a stretcher into a luggage-lift; to be told by a chatty porter – Beattie, it may have been – that though the gentleman was dead, the destination was Charing Cross Hospital, at the Trafalgar Square end of the Strand. Said Enani went straight back to his room. Either he didn't feel like talking to his mistress – ex-mistress now – or she, despite her peremptory telephone command, didn't want to see him. Not at the moment, at any rate, while she was talking to someone else. She had, you see, made an outside call to the available-at-all-hours Dr. Gordon, and (one wonders whether he slept in his black jacket and striped trousers) he had got to the suite in his usual double-quick time.

According to Gordon,

Madame Fahmy, in an excited state, explained to me in French that her husband had been ill-treating her that evening and that he had forced his attentions upon her; she also said that at supper he had threatened to smash her head in. She alleged that, when they were together in the suite, he had approached her and threatened her, and that she had fired her automatic pistol out of the window. She then thought the pistol was unloaded. When, later, her hus-band advanced, she fired the pistol and was surprised to hear a report. She lost her head when her husband fell, although she thought he was shamming. It was not until she saw blood that she realised what she had done. She said that when she fired one shot she did not know that another would come up into the magazine.

She gave Gordon the note cancelling whatever arrangements she had made with his specialist colleague; and she reminded him of comments she had made during his earlier visits, apropos of the cause and aggravation of her medical complaint – comments that I shall refer to later.

Gordon was still with her, and insisted on staying with her, when Detective Inspector Edward Grosse, with one or two officers of lower rank, arrived to investigate the shooting occurrence. Grosse was just the sort of detective that the Savoy might have ordered: smart but not dandy, taciturn, and quiet when he did speak; clearly not a paying guest of the hotel but possibly a paying guest's valet. Nice and unobtrusive.

Not nice to John Beattie, though. The porter – perhaps because he felt rather proprietorial about what had happened (over the next few days he would, strictly on the quiet, make more in tips – all from reporters – than he usually made in a year) or because he had been deputed to tidy up – had found three cartridge cases and a spent bullet, and stowed them in the hidy-hole in which he had already placed the gun that had discharged them. When he handed the collection to Grosse, far from being thanked, he was scolded for disarranging material evidence and getting his finger-prints all over it.

Grosse doesn't seem to have said anything to Madame Fahmy other than to ask her to accompany him to Bow Street Police Station. She went quietly. The only delay was sparked off by Dr. Gordon, who after insisting to Grosse that he was coming too, advised his patient to exchange her evening garb for daytime wear. Grosse waited in the corridor while she – unaided, for neither of her maids had been stirred – slipped out of her shimmering dress and put on (I quote from the *Daily Express*'s report of her appearance when she appeared, to be remanded in custody, in the police court next day) 'a black mushroom-shaped hat and a jade blouse beneath a black charmeuse coat' . . . or (going by the *Daily Graphic*'s account) attired herself in 'a long, dark satin coat, trimmed with brown fur at the neck, sleeves and round the bottom, a rope of tiny pearls round her neck, long dropped earrings, and glistening rings on each hand'.

Now comes an if not inexplicable, then distinctly odd hiatus of about two hours in Edward Grosse's night-shift. One must presume that he left one or more of his helpmates in the corridor; but that presumption does not extend to a belief that any investigating was done while he was away. Apart from arranging for two wardresses to be closeted with Madame Fahmy in a room at the police station, ensuring that Dr. Gordon was comfortable adjacently, and telling a constable to rustle up tea and biscuits for the lady and her leech, he seems to have been inactive till shortly before five o'clock, when he made his way down the Strand, passing the Savoy on his left, and turned right at Agar Street, making for the Charing Cross Hospital. There, he obtained written confirmation that Madame Fahmy was a widow. Then he went back to the Savoy:

> I examined the corridor of the fourth floor. I found a hole in the wall. It was the size of a bullet, and approximately three feet from the floor. Some yards farther on I found that the beading of a glass door had apparently recently been shot away, and I found a hole in the beading through which a bullet had passed. A dent somewhat similar to the other marks was found on the banisters at the top of the stairway.
>
> I then entered the suite of rooms where the victim and his wife were living, and found in the wife's room a white evening-dress adorned with white beads. The lower part of the garment was bloodstained. I then entered the victim's room, and found on the ground broken beads like those I saw on the wife's dress.

It was six o'clock when he finished his foraging. By that time, too, a photographer having taken shots of the scene of the crime, Grosse had given Arthur Mariani the go-ahead for the eradication of signs of the crime that might upset passing guests, and a number of chars, warned to work silently, were sponging and wiping outside the suite. After six, a statement was taken from Mariani; also from Thomas de Bich, John Beattie, and Said Enani.

Returning to the police station, Grosse asked after Madame Fahmy, and was told that she was sleeping. He arranged for a statement to be taken from Dr. Gordon. Perhaps because of delay in getting an interpreter, or perhaps because Grosse's mother had told him, as mine told me, that a lady's day should not begin before that of an office-worker, he waited till nine o'clock before asking for Madame Fahmy to be roused so that he might charge her with the murder of her husband.

According to the interpreter, she replied: 'I have told the police I did it. I told the truth. It does not matter. My husband has assaulted me in front of many people since we have been married. He has told me many times to kill him. I lost my head.'

On the dot of nine o'clock, Dr. Gordon made a phone call to the offices of Freke Palmer, who for close to a decade, ever since the naughty Arthur Newton had been struck off the roll of solicitors of the Supreme Court, had had the busiest criminal practice in the country. Palmer, as fast in responding to a call for assistance of the wealthy as was the good doctor, got to Bow Street, without looking as if he had hurried, shortly after Inspector Grosse had finished interviewing Madame Fahmy. Gordon effected an introduction between her and the solicitor, advised her that Palmer was the best of his kind that money could buy (calumnious to say this, I suppose, but I shouldn't be surprised if Gordon had fixed a cut from Palmer's fee), and withdrew.

Freke Palmer, having got the gist of his client's version of what had happened at the Savoy earlier that morning, and – as important – having taken in every mite of her black reminiscences of life with Ali, sat fairly quietly by her during the brief magisterial proceedings. He asked only two questions, both of Inspector Grosse – who replied, unpleasingly, to the first that the prisoner, when and after being charged, had 'seemed calm and collected, not at all hysterical,' and to the second that, yes, he *had* been told by Dr. Gordon that she had arranged to enter a nursing home for an operation that day. After saying that his client would reserve her defence, Palmer was granted the request that she be driven to Holloway Gaol, not in a black Maria, but in a hired limousine.

It would be interesting to know whether or not she received similarly special treatment – privacy from poorer remandees in the hospital block, for instance – after her admission to Holloway.

Expense was no object to Freke Palmer's briefing, hiring, tipping, and buying in aid of saving Madame Fahmy from either the sudden punishment of dislocation of her neck or a long term of imprisonment. As he had done many times before, he briefed the roly-poly, seemingly-genial Sir Henry Curtis-Bennett, whose fame as a defender in criminal cases was surpassed by only one other King's Counsel; also, he briefed the eminent junior counsel, the slim, saturnine Roland Oliver. In the previous December, those two barristers had been on opposing sides at the Old Bailey, the former leading the defence of Edith Thompson, the latter assisting the Crown to prove, so the jury decided, that Mrs Thompson and her young lover Frederick Bywaters were both guilty of her husband's murder. Palmer's pairing of Curtis-Bennett with Oliver was still red-hot news within the Inns of Court when he announced, astonishingly, that there was to be a third member of the defence team, a co-leader of it – none other than Sir Edward Marshall Hall, KC, the most famed defender of all time.

Never before had such a trio of forensic talents been assembled. A trio a trifle too starry, it seemed to some. Curtis-Bennett was an 'actor-barrister' (he once remarked that it might be a good thing if he had an orchestra to play soft music while he made the speech for the defence) – but his courtroom histrionics were delicate compared with those of Marshall Hall: if 'Curtis' was the Gerald Du Maurier of Theatre Royal, Old Bailey, then 'the Marshall' was its Henry Irving. Were they to share top billing for the defence at the Fahmy trial, the audience of jurors might, while being entranced by the double-act, feel that the defence case was all show and no substance.

That thought may have occurred, post-briefing, to Freke Palmer, causing him to request Curtis-Bennett to become, as it were, the director and prompter of a Marshall Hall solo performance; or perhaps Curtis-Bennett, assured of his fee whether he shared the advocacy or took a figurative back-seat, alongside Roland Oliver, decided not to risk being outshone. Either way, it was agreed that Marshall Hall should do all the acting at the trial; that Curtis-Bennett and Oliver should prepare his material – and learn their own lines based on it, so that in the event of his going so far 'over the top' that he required out-of-court medical aid, one or both of them, expensive understudies, could take over.

Early in the discussions between the solicitor and the barristers, a two-tier strategy was worked out. The jury would be asked to believe Madame Fahmy's statement that the shooting was a nasty accident – that, believing that her automatic pistol was empty, she had used it merely as a 'frightener', pointing it at the threateningly advancing Ali in the hope of halting his progress . . . and that when it had no such effect, she had instinctively clenched the trigger – and only released it after three completely unexpected shots had been fired. Even if the jury found that explanation not entirely implausible, they might return a verdict of manslaughter.

And so they had to be persuaded – probably contra to a warning by the judge that the concept of *crime passionnel* was not accepted excusingly under English law – that the defendant, tormented and sexually abused for months on end, eventually fearing that further outrage would endanger her life, had no choice but to kill her husband, a perverted Arab, lest he kill her.

The *no-intention* component of the defence case could be left to Marshall Hall, who was a dab-hand at firearms, and yet more expert at making juries accept *his* science of ballistics in preference to that of firearms experts called by the Crown: he would get his friend George Stopp, manager of Whistler's gun-shop in the Strand, to cram him with the ins and outs of the Browning .25 automatic pistol, which was the type of weapon used by Madame Fahmy (one of a matching pair, His and Hers, that the Fahmys always kept by their bedsides) – and then, if he couldn't make the firing of one – *two* – **three** bullets seem unintended, no advocate could.

As for the *no-choice* component, every effort would be made, many back-handers paid, to create a warts-and-all (the 'and-all' redundant to the purpose) picture of Prince Ali Kamel Fahmy Bey. Ex-employees of his would be traced, tempted, quizzed; a firm of private investigators in Cairo, and another in Paris, would be engaged to ferret for uncomplimentary information about him.

Madame Fahmy's defenders had one large dilemma. It concerned her ailment – that which, as you will recall, she had planned to have surgical treatment for. The ailment, so she had told Dr. Gordon before the shooting and Freke Palmer afterwards, had been caused by her husband, and made worse, till the discomfort was fierce, by his continuance of the pastime that had caused it. The knotty problem for her defenders was composed of the following strands:

They wanted her to be seen as A Romantic Figure – but if the name of her complaint were revealed, it would, like a spot of ink on blotting paper, spread pretentiously, obsessing observers of her and casting all thoughts of Romance from their minds; on the other hand, her terror that Ali, creator and exciter of the complaint, intended imminently to pleasure himself, no matter how she was thereby pained, gave her a motive for killing him – or at least incapacitating him – that no one, not even a dedicated masochist, could possibly look down upon; but the trouble there was that Ali's pleasurable pursuit was even more unmentionable than the complaint that Madame Fahmy blamed upon it; and suppose that if the defence hired the leading euphemist and, having accepted his discreet advice, spoke of the unspeakable at the trial, there was the fearful danger that the jury, not quite cottoning on, would think that, just as it took two to tango, Ali and his wife had been consenting partners in the pursuit, she deriving nearly as much pleasure from it as did he, prior to the onset of the resultant ailment.

Having weighed the pros and cons, the defenders agreed that both the pursuit and the complaint had to be skirted.

I think that now, in an age when outspokenness is expected by most people and practised like a profession by those who have little to speak of that is worth hearing about, it is all right to say that the pursuit was sodomy, the ailment haemorrhoids, otherwise called piles. As one or two specially gentle readers may appreciate a moment to recover from those disclosures, I shall leave a space.

The trial of Madame Fahmy occupied Number One Court in the Old Bailey for six days, from ten o'clock on the morning of Monday, 10 September – exactly two months since she had been charged and cautioned by, and had made a statement to, Detective Inspector Grosse. Her judge was Mr. Justice Rigby Swift, who is recalled by Edward Spencer Shew, for years a court reporter, in his good reference book, *A Companion to Murder* (London, 1960):

> One [hears] in one's fancy the drawling voice, with its flattened vowel sounds, the short 'a', the tones which suggested, rather than reproduced, the speech of his native Lancashire, above all the peculiar habit he had of elongating the final syllable of certain words and then snapping if off, explosively. (The very word 'remember' recalls this trick. On the lips of Mr. Justice Swift it would be certain to come out as 'remem-*bah*'. This mannerism was so well known in the Temple that lawyers used to refer to him – and still do – as 'Rig-*bah*'.) One needs to remember, also, how he looked as he sat on the Bench; the round, rubicund face under the bob wig, the glowing cheeks, the nose like a button, the amiable lift of the mouth, the bright, observant eyes, the endearing air of *bonhomie*. And all the various tricks and mannerisms which were so much a part of the man need to be remembered, too – such as the habit of slowly tapping his pencil three times upon the desk before him as a warning that he was about to say something apt and shrewd, and frequently devastating. (At those premonitory taps, much to his delight, an awful silence would descend upon the court.)

The leading Crown counsel was Percival Clarke, the eldest son of a greater advocate.

There were two women on the jury.

And, every day, as many women as men contributed to the crowding of the public spaces – shamefully, in the view of 'A Psychologist', paid by the *Daily Express* to sit in the no less crowded Press pen:

> The woman spectator . . . seeks entertainment from the wreck of some other life, and she sits through the most revolting evidence outwardly placid, inwardly indulging in an orgy of unhealthy sensation. . . . [At the Fahmy trial, women] sit and nod to their friends with the self-satisfied smirk of those who enjoy privileges not granted to less influential persons. Among them was more than one matron accompanied by a girl who appeared not be be of the age to vote at the polling booths.
>
> The study of their faces was a lesson in feminine psychology. The more unprintable the evidence brought forward, the more they rejoiced in listening to it. . . .

The two women who *had* to be present, Madame Fahmy and a wardress ('whose neat and kindly personality suggested' – to the *Daily Graphic*'s reporter – 'a ministering angel of the V[oluntary] A[id] D[etachment]'), had ample elbow-room, for the dock in the main Central Criminal Court was large enough to accommodate a score of burly men. The defendant dressed differently each day; though it was at least two months since she had bought any clothes, she always looked fashionable.

Before the indictment was read, the judge gave permission for an interpreter – one of two, working turn and turn about – to sit near Madame Fahmy. The interpreter's first task was to put into French the Clerk's question, whether she was guilty or innocent of the murder of her husband. '*Non coupable*,' she replied – quietly but sounding as though she meant what she said. If she was capable of relaxing, she was allowed to do so for the rest of that day and the whole of the next: she would not be asked further questions till Wednesday morning.

After Percival Clarke had outlined the case for the prosecution, a few minor witnesses gave evidence. Then came the second Big Moment: the calling of Said Enani – 'a short dapper figure in a well-tailored blue suit' (*Daily Express*). It came as a surprise to him, though he didn't show it, that the first questions he was asked came, not from Clarke, examining-in-chief, but from Marshall Hall. No sooner had he taken the oath than defence counsel rose – majestic and as awe-inspiring as an eagle in his black gown – and demanded to know:

'On what book were you sworn?'

'The Bible.'

'Does the oath on the Bible bind you?'

'Yes.'

The judge intervened: 'You regard an oath taken on the Gospels as binding on your conscience?'

'Yes, sir.'

Rigby Swift twitched his eyebrows at Marshall Hall, wondering if he was satisfied. And the latter sighed hugely, shrugged extravagantly, shook his lovely head at the jury, and sagged back into his pew. He had scored thrice – by raising a doubt about the witness's veracity, by putting him off his stroke, by treating the jurors, all twelve of them, as allies.

Freke Palmer had brought from Cairo, and was treating royally, either as kings or queens, two exquisite young men who had been intimates of Ali. The couple, each daintily coiffured and cosmeticised, flanked the solicitor in unwitting mimicry of porcelain bookends when, directly after the luncheon adjournment, Said Enani stood in the witness box, waiting to be cross-examined. Keeping him waiting a while longer, Marshall Hall turned to Palmer, whispered something, then bowed to each of the Egyptians. His intention was to ensure that Said Enani noticed the young men and associated them with the defence; his hope was that the secretary would be influenced to speak with some candour about aspects of his dead master's social life by the belief that loyal reticence was pointless, since gaps in his testimony would be filled by the young men, defence witnesses to be. Actually, Marshall Hall did not mean to call them; they had been pumped by the defence, and were now just intimidatory props; as soon as Said Enani had left the witness box, they would be shipped back to Egypt, the chinking of their trinkets accompanied by the clinking of pieces of silver from Palmer's petty-cash box.

It is hard to make out whether or not the intimidatory ploy worked. During the four hours of the cross-examination, Said Enani rarely feigned ignorance of matters that must have been within his knowledge – but his stated recollections were less dramatic than the defence would have liked; as each question was put to him, his mind started censoring the whole-truth answer that he had sworn to tell. That was no bad thing for the defence: so long as a person being cross-examined consistently diminishes the truth, sensible members of the jury will amend all the footnote-size answers to a larger fount, perhaps of bold type. Marshall Hall had to be careful that, in attacking Ali's character, he delivered no more than glancing blows against that of the witness: an overt attempt to discredit him would bring into play the tit-for-tat rule of legal combat, entitling the prosecution to 'dish the dirt' about the defendant. Marshall Hall's first few questions were risky, and one wouldn't be surprised if Curtis-Bennett, sitting next to him, sent up a nose-blowing, brief-riffling or even gown-tugging signal, causing him to change the subject.

Q. How long did you know Fahmy?

A. For seven years.

Q. Before he came into his money, you lived together?

A. No.

Q. He had no money then? He was poor?

A. He had £100 a month.

Q. What was your employment at that time?

A. I was employed by the Minister of the Interior.

Q. At what salary?

A. £22 a month.

Q. And when you became Fahmy's private secretary, was there a clause in the agreement providing that you should be paid at £35 a month for ten years' service, whether you served all that time or not?

A. That is so.

The best instance of Said Enani's diminished responses is his answer to a question, one of several, regarding Ali's physical ill-treatment of the defendant: whereas Marshall Hall spoke of 'a heavy blow across the face', the witness preferred 'a smack'.

He recalled, but in faint light, many of the public arguments and fights between the Fahmys. There was, for example, an incident during the prior-to-London stay in Paris:

Q. Following a visit to the Folies Bergères, did Fahmy seize her by the throat?

A. I do not know that. I did see him take off a bracelet which she had given him and throw it at her.

Q. On that occasion I suggest that she was bleeding from the mouth from a blow given by her husband?

A. I remember a small mark near her nose.

Switching from the particular to the general, Marshall Hall asked: 'Was he a bully?'

A. He was rather shy.

Q. You know what 'a bully' means? Was he a man in the habit of beating women – not only one woman, but women?

A. No, sir. He would dispute with them, but I have never seen him beat them.

Q. You have known of his intimacies with many women?

A. Yes, sir.

Q. Do you know that he treated them brutally, one and all?

A. No, sir; I cannot say brutally.

Near the end of the day, Marshall Hall referred, for the first and only time during the cross-examination, to Madame Fahmy's plan to enter a nursing home for an operation. He suggested that Said Enani had heard his master tell her to 'go to the devil' when she broached the subject.

A. I do not recall his saying that.

Q. Was she always crying?

A. No.

Q. Was the Madame Fahmy of 1923 totally different from the Madame Laurent of 1922?

A. Perhaps – but she did not cry.

Q. Had every bit of life been crushed out of her during those six months?

A. I do not know.

Q. From an entertaining and fascinating woman, had she become miserable and wretched?

A. They were always quarrelling.

Q. And did she say that you and Fahmy were always against her, and that it was a case of two against one?

A. Yes.

Q. Did you say that if she would give you £2000, you would clear out of her way?

A. I said that if she would discharge me, I should be pleased to go. I did not say anything about money.

Q. Did you give her presents?

A. Yes; but they were not expensive.

Q. At supper on the night of the tragedy, did he say, 'I will disfigure you so that no one else will want you'?

A. I do not remember.

To preface his last question, a risky one, Marshall Hall produced an enlarged copy of a cartoon that had appeared in a Cairo magazine called *Kachkoul*, which seems to have been an Arabian forerunner, more satirical, of *Private Eye*. The drawing was of three profiles, each of two of them set back from the one below, and the caption read: 'The Light, the Shadow of the Light, and the Shadow of the Shadow of the Light.' The topmost profile was of Fahmy, the next of Said Enani, and the bottom one of the secretary's own secretary.

'I suggest,' Marshall Hall thundered, 'that the association between yourself and Fahmy was notorious in Egypt.'

'That is not so,' Said Enani replied softly.

Still scowling at him, Marshall Hall sat down.

Percival Clarke was on his feet at once – not to re-examine but to protest to the judge that the cartoon that had been flourished to his entire surprise reflected on the witness's moral character.

Patting a yawn, Rigby Swift responded, 'It does not reflect on anybody's moral character – except, perhaps, the artist's,' and before Clarke could say another word, adjourned the proceedings till the following day . . .

. . . when 'the other Mr. Churchill' – Robert, the gunsmith of Agar Street, off the Strand – gave evidence. Macdonald Hastings, who wrote Churchill's biography (London, 1963), says that the gunsmith's appearance at the trial

> was a routine affair. Madame Fahmy admitted that the pistol was hers, and that she had fired the shots – whether intentionally or otherwise it was for the court to decide – which had killed her husband.
>
> But Marshall Hall, partly because the winking mechanism of a gun fascinated him in the same way that he was fascinated by jewellery, partly because it was most important to his case to impress the jury that he knew more about firearms than anyone else in court, used his friend Churchill in a subtle way to underline the reasonableness of the case he was planning to make. Cross-examining him in the witness box, he got Churchill to explain the workings of an automatic pistol; how for the purpose of emptying a loaded cartridge out of the breech it was necessary to pull back the breech cover to dribble it out. He suggested that a person inexperienced in firearms – as most women are – might not know this,

might think that to empty the gun the only way was to fire the round in the barrel; indeed, might well be ignorant of the fact that, in an automatic, the recoil of one round lifts another round out of the magazine into the firing position. Churchill agreed that that was true.

For the defence it was a little step forward. One shot, out of the three that had to be explained away, had been accounted for; providing, that is, that the prosecution didn't pooh-pooh the suggestion by pointing out that the pistol was Madame Fahmy's personal property, not her husband's, and that it was unlikely, if not highly improbable, that a woman who thought it necessary to have a pistol for the protection of her jewels wouldn't have taken the trouble to find out how it worked.

Churchill was one of a number of men from the neighbourhood of the Strand who appeared as prosecution witnesses that day. The others were – in ascending order of importance at the Savoy – John Beattie, Arthur Mariani, and Thomas de Bich. And Dr. Edward Gordon – who, having answered questions from Percival Clarke about, among other things, his after-the-shooting consultation with Madame Fahmy, was asked by the judge:

'Did Madame Fahmy explain what she meant by her husband having brutally handled her immediately prior to the tragedy?'

'She told me that he took her by the arms in the bedroom.' (But *which* bedroom? *Hers?* – as she stated, through an interpreter, to Inspector Grosse when he interviewed her at the police station. Or *her husband's?* – as may have been indicated by Grosse's earlier observation of crushed white beads on the floor by Fahmy's bedside.)

The doctor's reply to the judge's question left Percival Clarke with no choice but to ask: 'Did you see any marks of bruising on her arms?'

'She showed me a scratch on the back of her neck, about an inch and a half long, probably caused by a fingernail. She said it was caused by her husband.' Adding to Clarke's misery, Gordon added: 'When I saw her on 4 July [six days before the day he had been asked about], she had bruises on her arm and leg, which she said had been caused by her husband "fighting her".'

Cross-examining, Marshall Hall asked: 'Was the mark on the neck consistent with a hand clutching at her throat?' And was delighted with the positive reply, the unrequested, ideally-worded addenda: 'It was. Madame Fahmy complained that her husband was very passionate, and that his conduct had made her ill. Her condition was consistent with conduct she alleged against him.'

With a little help from friendly witnesses like Gordon, Marshall Hall had already given excellent value for the 652 guineas marked on his brief.[1] His speech to introduce the case for the defence made the sum inadequate (and, as will appear, his closing speech, on its own, was deserving of more than any other barrister has ever been paid). He began the opening speech at three o'clock on the Tuesday afternoon, and, careful with the timing, only sat down when he saw the judge looking at the clock in a wistful-for-adjournment way. During the speech, he referred to Madame Fahmy's contention that the shooting was accidental – but devoted most of his efforts to making the jury think that if ever a man had deserved to be killed, that man was her husband:

'Fahmy Bey, shortly before he was shot, attacked his wife like a raving, lustful beast because she would not agree to an outrageous suggestion he made – a suggestion which would fill every decent-minded person with utter revulsion. Almost throughout their miserably tragic life of six months, this treacherous Egyptian beast pursued his wife with this unspeakable request, and because she – immoral though she may have been – resisted him, he heaped cruelty and brutality on her until she was changed, by fear, from a charming, attractive woman to a poor quaking creature hovering on the brink of nervous ruin.'

First thing next day, the jury's entrance was delayed while Percival Clarke submitted to the judge that he should be allowed 'to dispel the idea that the defendant was a poor child dominated over by this man'. He went on to explain: 'I want to prove that she associated with men from an early age, and that she is a woman of the world in the widest sense. I submit that I am entitled to ask her how she treated other men. I do not want it to be thought that all the fault was on the husband's side.'

Mr. Justice Swift: 'Sir Edward [Marshall Hall] has said that she was an immoral woman, but he said it in such a way that he gave

[1] If Curtis-Bennett's fee was in the same region, and supposing that Roland Oliver was receiving the usual fee to a junior of two-thirds of that of leading King's Counsel, the bill for the three defenders (excluding any 'refreshers' that were paid to them) amounted, in present-day terms, to about £25,000.

the impression to everyone who listened to his speech that she was an innocent and most respectable woman. It is a difficult thing to do, but Sir Edward, with all that skill we have admired for so long, has done it.' Rigby Swift then seemed to contradict himself by ruling against Clarke's submission. Marshall Hall must have thought to himself, 'Hoorah, Rigbah,' or something to that effect.

Once the jurors were settled, he requested Madame Fahmy to leave the dock and go to the witness box – which she did, so unsteadily that her VAD chaperone needed to give her a hand. Till now, the spectators in the gallery had looked exhausted and bedraggled, for they had had to queue for their slight spaces since before two in the morning; but the progress of the prisoner perked them to become as one, an oblong of unblemished alertness, an organ that went ooh and ah, that throbbed with expectancy.

I hate to say this – and not because I have it in me to feel sorrow for the spectators – but the show did not live up to advance publicity. Everything would have been fine if only Madame Fahmy had bothered to learn English in the period between her arrest and the trial. But no: she still couldn't even say please or thank-you. And so every single question put to her was followed by the rigmarole of translation of it into French by an interpreter, her answer in that language, the interpreter's English version of what she had said. Tedious.

And irritating to those who believed that there was such a thing as the *whole* truth – for the word-structure of a witness's reply is sometimes almost or as revealing as the meaning of the reply; and, of course, there was the chance of a forensic variation on the military tale of the message to 'send reinforcements, we are going to advance' that, muddled by middlemen, finished up at HQ as 'send three and fourpence, we are going to a dance'. Why, even the oath-taking ceremony was unsatisfactory. Marshall Hall had queried Said Enani's acceptance of the Bible – but when Madame Fahmy used the same volume, no one for the prosecution pointed out that, unless a Holloway-visiting priest had officially returned her to Catholicism, she was still a Moslem . . . and that, in any event, it was surely unsafe to assume that she considered herself bound by an oath on a book of words, *sans* that of *Dieu*, that were complete gibberish to her.

Going by the translations of her answers, she stuck pretty much to her story as we know it. In cross-examining her, Percival Clarke achieved only a few, minor successes. For instance, she had agreed with Marshall Hall that she had been 'terrorised' by several of Ali's employees, including a black valet – but she had to admit to Clarke that the valet was a youth of eighteen who was only five feet tall.

She quite often wept, and once or twice swooned. The big dramatic moment was during examination-in-chief, when Marshall Hall asked that a pistol like her own be handed to her. The *Daily Express*:

> The drooping, slim figure in black, almost hidden in the witness box, rose slowly, and a small black-gloved hand stretched out to take the pistol held over the ledge of the witness box by the court usher.
>
> Then in a flash, the small gloved hand recoiled as if it had been touched by an electric current, and was pressed over two tear-rimmed eyes in which revulsion flashed. The pistol fell on the ledge of the witness box, and in the tense silence it seemed that some great weight had crashed on the wood.
>
> 'Come, Madame Fahmy, take hold of the pistol; it is harmless now,' came Sir Edward Marshall Hall's soft voice reassuringly across the court, and the small black-gloved hand of the trembling woman in the witness box closed on the pistol.

The questioning of her went on throughout Wednesday, and was continued next day, till about noon. Between that time and the luncheon recess, three other defence witnesses were heard.

First, Yvonne Alibert, the defendant's sister, who said that, during the Fahmys' visit to Paris, she had seen bruises on Madame Fahmy's face and body, and had heard her husband threaten her. She added that, prior to the visit, she had received two letters from Ali: 'I regarded them as improper. In one letter he asked me to place his love at the feet of a lady who was in Paris, and requested me to become acquainted with nice women so that he might be introduced to them.'

Second, Amy Pain, Madame Fahmy's maid, who remembered thaat, 'on one occasion, when Madame wished to wear an evening dress at Luxor, she had to use a great deal of cream and powder to hide the bruises on her neck and back'. Amy created a stir in court – and a collective shudder of defenders – by tagging on to one of her answers a recollection that she had never mentioned before – 'because I was so upset. Between eight and nine on the night of the tragedy, I heard a shot, and saw Madame Fahmy put a pistol on the arm of a chair.' Perhaps because, clearly, she was wrong about the time (by eight o'clock, the Fahmys, with Said Enani, were watching, if not enjoying, *The Merry Widow*), Percival Clarke did not express interest.

Third, Eugene Barbay, auxiliary chauffeur to the Fahmys in Paris, who, as well as commenting on 'Madame's bruises', recalled that during an argument between his master and mistress, the former had said – well, had said *something*. The interpreter declined to interpret, explaining between blushes that 'the certain expression is so bad that even in court it cannot be uttered'. Coaxed by Rigby Swift, the interpreter gave a clue: 'It is usually indicated by an initial' – but refused point-blank to narrow the possibilities from twenty-six.

On that demure note, the morning session ended.

Straightway after lunch, Marshall Hall began the greatest defending speech of his life.

Having sought to simplify things for the jury by telling them, 'Either this was a deliberate, premeditated and cowardly murder, or it was a shot fired by this woman from a pistol which she believed was unloaded at a moment when she thought her life was in danger,' he used racism in what he believed was a good cause:

'She made one great mistake,' he said quietly – 'possibly the greatest mistake any woman of the West *can* make. She married an Oriental.'

A pause to allow that thought to sink in; then, still quietly, he went on:

'I dare say the Egyptian civilisation is one of the oldest and most wonderful in the world. I do not say that among the Egyptians there are not many magnificent and splendid men. But if you strip off the external civilisation of the Oriental, you have the real Oriental underneath – and it is common knowledge that the Oriental's treatment of women does not fit in with the idea the Western woman has of the way she should be treated by her husband.'

After suggesting that Said Enani epitomised 'Eastern duplicity', and asking the jury if they did not think that Madame Fahmy had reason to fear 'Hercules, the great black blackguard who owed his life to Fahmy', Marshall Hall reverted to the never-the-twain theme:

'The curse of this case is the atmosphere of the East which we cannot understand – the Eastern feeling of possession of the woman, the Turk in his harem. This man Fahmy was entitled to have four wives if he liked. For chattels. Which to us Western people, with our ideas of women, is almost unintelligible – something we cannot deal with.

'Picture this woman, inveigled into Egypt by false pretences – by letters which for adulatory expression could hardly be equalled. *And which make one feel SICK*. At first, everything is honey and roses. He shows her his beautiful palace, his costly motor-cars, his wonderful motor-boat, his retinue of servants, his lavish luxuries, and cries, 'Ah, I am Fahmy Bey – I am a prince!'

There was more, much more, along much the same lines: contempt for Ali – for all but a few Orientals, for virtually the entire adult male population of Egypt. (Following the trial, the Attorney-General received a long cable of protest from the Bâtonnier of the Egyptian Bar, the Foreign and Colonial Secretaries had to placate ambassadors and high commissioners from places east of Greece – and Marshall Hall was persuaded to write, or put his signature to, a letter saying that he hadn't said any of the anti-Oriental things that he had said.)

When Mr. Justice Swift adjourned the proceedings – earlier than usual – on the Thursday, Marshall Hall had not finished. Continuing the speech next morning, he cheekily told the jury: 'While your decision must not be governed by sympathy, still less must it be governed by prejudice.' Then he got angry with Percival Clarke for having framed a question to Robert Churchill in such a way as to suggest that if Madame Fahmy really had fired her pistol out of the hotel window before the shooting, she had done so not with the intention of rendering it harmless but to make sure that it was in working order: 'The suggestion is that this wicked woman, this murderess, shot her husband like a dog. I regret – I reject – that suggestion, because there is absolutely nothing but the suggestion.' Calming himself, he whispered a description of the thunderstorm. Then:

'Imagine its effect on a woman of nervous temperament who had been living such a life as she had lived for the past six months – outraged . . . abused . . . beaten . . . degraded.' Grasping a pistol – it may have been the real one – he went into a crouch; no one in court had much doubt that it was the crouch of a stealthy Oriental, but Marshall Hall confirmed this by explaining, 'In sheer desperation –

as he crouched for the last time, crouched like an animal, like an Oriental, retired for the last time to get a bound forward – she turned the pistol and put it to his face. And . . . to her horror . . . the thing went off.'

While speaking, he had pointed the pistol towards the jury.

Now he dropped it.

The clatter as it hit the floor and bounced was not that at all to the people in court. To them it was a series of explosions. And as Marshall Hall, no longer crouching, crooned, 'Sweetheart, speak to me!', he was a translated Madame Fahmy to a T.

Himself again, he roared: 'Was that deliberate murder? Would she choose the Savoy Hotel for such an act?'

'No,' shrilled a woman in the gallery. 'Of course not,' another, more talkative, piped up.

Coming towards the end of his act, Marshall Hall spoke of 'that wonderful work of fiction by Robert Hichens, *Bella Donna*,' and continued:

'You will remember the final scene, where this woman goes out of the gates of the garden into the dark night of the desert. Members of the jury, I want you to open the gates where this Western woman can go out – not into the dark night of the desert but back to her friends, who love her in spite of her weaknesses; back to her friends, who will be glad to receive her; back to her child, who will be waiting for her with open arms.'

Right on cue, a shaft of sunlight pierced the glass dome of the court. Pointing his whole hand at it, Marshall Hall ordered the jury: 'You will open the gate and let this Western woman go back into the light of God's great Western sun.'

Then he sat down; almost fell down, having taken so much out of himself.

There was no applause. Or rather, there was that greatest of all applause, which is utter silence.

Poor Percival Clarke, having to speak next, showed, at least, that he had attended better to *Bella Donna* than had Marshall Hall. The work was, he said, 'a strangely unfortunate one to recall to mind. The woman who went out into the desert, out into the dark, was the woman who planned and nearly succeeded in murdering her husband. In that respect, it may be that the simile between the work and this case is somewhat close.' The main thrust of Clarke's speech seems to have been towards reminding the jury that they were 'trying the woman in the dock, not the dead man'.

Late in the afternoon, Mr. Justice Swift began to sum up, commenting that he had been 'shocked, sickened and disgusted' by some of the evidence. Continuing next morning, he told the jury that they had to decide on one of three verdicts: guilt of murder or of manslaughter, or innocence; but he gave no clues to which of the verdicts he considered most apt.

The jury retired just before half-past noon, and returned a minute or so after half-past one. The foreman had to speak loudly to make the words 'Not guilty' audible above the weepy moans of one of the jurywomen, the drama too much for her, and the stentorian soothing of her by the stiff-upper-lipped other.

Madame Fahmy must have taught herself at least one English word, that being 'not'. Prior to the foreman's utterance of it, she stood with her elbows on the rail of the dock, her hands giving further cover to her veiled face – but the moment the word came out, her fingers pinched the muslin and flicked it atop her cloche, revealing a beaming face.

There was great rejoicing in the gallery: the cheers, whoops, screams and shouts made a din loud enough to be heard by the hundreds of Madame Fahmy fans blocking the street outside, and the resultant racket from them could be heard in the courtroom like an echo of the galleryites' delight. Outraged, Rigby Swift snarled an order for all spectators, including the few unhysterical ones, to be removed. Once the only sounds were external, he said to the interpreter (a French woman barrister who had replaced a regular interpreter at Marshall Hall's request): 'Tell the defendant that the jury have found her not quilty and that she is discharged.'

The translation of those words had a bad effect on Madame Fahmy: the joyfulness dwindled from her features and she swayed as if about to swoon. There were two wardresses in the dock today, and they both grabbed the woman who was no longer in their charge, volte-faced her, and half-carried her down the steps to a reception room – where Dr. Gordon revived her with the aid of a jolter more expensive, to his patients, than sal-volatile. Though she was soon all right, she accepted advice not to leave the building for an hour – during which time, it was reckoned (rightly, as it turned out), the rabble would disperse. When she eventually slipped out of a side-door and into a waiting cab, only reporters and a few other people, desperate to see her or with nothing better to do, noticed her going. Either appropriately or quite inappropriately, her destination was the Prince's Hotel, smaller and smarter than the Savoy, in Jermyn Street.

There, instead of taking an *après*-ordeal *sieste*, she gave an audience to a 'special representative' of the Sunday paper that had made the winning bid in Freke Palmer's auction of her first EXCLUSIVE INTERVIEW. The journalist, bashful compared with most of his or her kind,

'. . . hesitated to disturb Mme. Fahmy in view of her wrought condition. But she was so glad to meet me that I felt she would be offended had I neglected the chance, on behalf of the readers of *The People*, to give her a word of sympathy and encouragement. "You may stay with me for five minutes," she said in her delightful French.' (One wonders if the translation is complete. Did she also point out that *The People* had purchased only five-minutes'-worth of her time and that a servant had already started a stop-watch?)

'Giving me her tiny hand, she invited me, with a wan smile, to sit and talk to her. Her room was glowing with colour. There were the choicest of flowers everywhere – a tribute from the enormous number of her compatriots, as well as English folk, who did not hesitate to show their sympathy in her trying hour. There were many mascots, too, sent by people of all classes as a magic solace.

'Madame told me she is not leaving London yet. "My doctor absolutely forbids me to travel, and so I must be patient," she said.' (Was Gordon nearby, nodding frantically, fondling his wallet the while?)

'Her wonderful eyes grew dim with tears as visions arose before her of the dreadful past. "Marriages between East and West can hardly ever turn out happily," she said.

'Madame Fahmy spoke of the splendid encouragement she had received from many unknown English women and girls in all stations in life. "They are like the mountains that look cold and stately with the white snow on them – white, like their English skin, but they are full of fire."

'When the possibility of her receiving a large fortune from her husband's estate was broached, she said the subject was painful and distasteful to her.' (So painful and distasteful that, though the *People*'s person still had a few seconds to go, she shut up like a clam.)

'As I bade adieu to this pathetic woman, she sank back with a sigh among the luxurious cushions on her couch.'

The size of Madame Fahmy's portion of the estate of the man whom she had, maybe unintentionally, punctured with three bullets was never revealed: not by her; nor by any member of either of the packs of civil lawyers – hers and the Fahmy family's – that, after a deal of dickering, one with the other, came to 'an equitable agreement'. If her negotiators were unworthy of their fees, and she got only the basic widow's entitlement, under Egyptian law, of one-sixth of the estate, it meant that her annual income was increased by not less than £8000 (now £112,000).

Reasonable compensation, or not, for nine months of different sorts of suffering? Making it all worth while?

I don't know the answers – but, in pondering the questions, I found a meaning of an old Gaelic saying that had perplexed me previously: *He* (or she) *that eats a slice of his* (or her) *spouse may, with great propriety, relish the soup that is made of the same.*

There is another unanswered question – to me, more tantalising than all the others posed by Madame Fahmy. For a few days following her trial, she was busy in the West End of London: party-going and interview-giving – and, it is nice to know, finding the time to pop in to see Marshall Hall at his chambers in the Inner Temple as well as sending him brief messages expressing her gratitude. Then she went to Paris; where, of course, she received a heroine's welcome. After two or three years, press stories about her doings appeared, not on news pages, but, aptly, in gossip columns; then, after a couple more years, the dropping of her name seems to have ceased. Is she, nonagenarian since 1980, still alive? If she is dead, the fact of it seems to have escaped the notice of journalists in both France and England. I have scanned newspaper indexes without coming across a reference to Madame Fahmy's demise; and, on my behalf, the librarian for a Fleet Street paper and the keeper of the morgue of a Paris one have looked in their respective *Fahmy* files – neither fruitfully.

There are several possible solutions to the Mystery of the Missing Obituary. The one I prefer, because it is the most romantic, is that Marguerite and Charles Laurent recreated their mutual love – with such effect on her heartstrings that she agreed to follow him to the Japanese end of the earth. And there she lived with him – calling herself Madame Laurent, perhaps: anyway, not Madame Fahmy – till he or she died. Her death, whether before or after his, might have got a mention in the local paper – but only because of her relationship with a renowned Japanophile. Nothing to do with an incident on the fourth floor back of the Savoy Hotel, London, England, during a thunderstorm that my father and some others who were kept awake by it would recall whenever the weather became inclement.

Postscript

At about nine o'clock on the tranquil night of Wednesday, 1 October 1980, a young man – slim, dark, with curly hair cascading over the collar of the trendy garment he was wearing rather than a jacket – booked into the Savoy Hotel; for that purpose, he called himself D. Richards, and claimed that he hailed from the Handsworth district of Birmingham. The booking clerk allotted him single-room No. 853, and mentioned – in the casual, but prepared to blame inflation, manner prescribed by his trainer – that the charge was £78 a night. (Comparatively speaking, not exorbitant: now the lowest charge is in three figures.)

At 10.15, a female employee of the hotel, doing something or other in a room on the eighth floor, was alarmed by screams issuing from room 853. She peeped into the corridor and saw a man – his trendy garb stippled with blood – emerge from room 853 and enter a lift. She waited till the position-indicator by the lift glowed G, then scampered along the corridor, pushed open the door of room 853, and looked within. What she saw caused her to make noises not unlike those that had made her curious. As a result, security men arrived; and one of them, shocked into forgetfulness of priorities, telephoned the police prior to speaking to an hotel executive.

Room 853 would need extensive redecoration, partial refurnishing, and entire replacement of the wall-to-wall carpeting.

The corpse of the woman who had screamed was lying near the bed. It was only partly clothed. An inventory of the garments on the body and lying about showed that when the woman had entered the room, some time after nine, she was wearing a white skirt and – each item black – a jumper, a sort of brassiere, a suspender-belt, fishnet stockings, and high-heeled shoes. And she was carrying a large black handbag made of glistening stuff called, inappropriately, Leatherlike.

This, too, was part of the mess. And so was something that, presumably, had come out of the bag: a wig of black hair, far more luxuriant than that of the dead woman. Among the paraphernalia still in the bag were articles indicating that it belonged to Ms Catherine Russell of 729 Chelsea Cloisters, SW3. Until the blood from fifty-five stab-wounds in the dead woman's body had been wiped away, it was difficult to make out whether a snapshot in the bag was of her; but that turned out to be so. The Savoy's PR people heaved small sighs of relief when early press reports of the crime referred to the victim as a masseuse; the relief was short lived, though, for subsequent reports noted that massage was but one of several skills, to say nothing of knacks, that Ms Russell, aged twenty-seven when she died, had practised upon or simply displayed to male clients, to the evident satisfaction of the great majority, during a career in prostitution that had stemmed from a pastime that she had indulged in, just for fun, when she was teenaged.

Room 853 contained not only clues to the identity of the victim but also clues to that of the culprit. A clasp-knife – one of those with a superfluity of accessories – lay, with its four-inch blade exposed, just inside the door. The whole contraption was smothered in blood, and the blood on the handle was dabbed with fingerprints. A tribute to the housemaid: when the polished tops of tables were examined, few fingerprints were found, but nearly all matched those on the handle of the knife. A further clue – a rather good one, this – was a pocket diary. The entries were of less interest to the police than a preliminary page, printed like a form and completed in pencil by the diarist:

NAME	*Tony Marriott*
HOME ADDRESS	*XX Highland Avenue,*
	Horsham, Sussex
EMPLOYER	(blank)
AGE	*Twenty-two*

– and so on, right down to collar-size, name and address of next-of-kin, National Insurance number. Fingerprints on the diary matched those already mentioned.

Soon after the arrival of the first policemen, one of them returned to the foyer and commandeered as evidence the registration book (the handwriting of the man who had signed in as D.

Richards was similar to that in the diary); he also quizzed the booking clerk, ascertained that Tony Marriott, alias D. Richards, had not settled his bill, and enquired of foyer staff and porters whether they had noticed a conspicuously bloodstained man leaving the hotel at about 10.15 (none had).

Marriott's movements after he walked out of the Savoy would be pieced together as follows: turning right, he hurried along the brightly-lit and crowded Strand, crossed it, and proceeded up Kingsway and onwards, till he reached the President Hotel, next to the Imperial, in *Russell* Square. The President's booking clerk – a short-sighted or unparticular individual, it seems – accepted the bloodstained, dishevelled and breathless man as a guest. Marriott must have been carrying a spare knife, for after entering the room allotted to him on the fourth floor, he tried to cut his left wrist, and then, having failed to pierce the artery, tried to cut his right wrist, but again without the determination that his apparent purpose required. Next day, he quit the President, without paying his bill, and travelled to Liverpool Street railway station, where he boarded a train to the Essex resort of Southend-on-Sea. In the evening, he visited the Britannia public house on the Esplanade.

The bloodstains, dried and dark by now, might have been taken by some for intended embellishments of trendy clothes – but the landlord of the Britannia, a middle-aged, untrendy man named James Locke, peered at them, raised his gaze to the customer's face, thought that it was a bit like a photograph of a face that he had seen on a televised news programme, and decided that he had better ring the police. Thus it was that Tony Marriott's post-murder Odyssey ended.

He admitted – no: insisted – that he had killed Catherine Russell. Musing in an interview room, he murmured, confusingly to the listeners: 'The real problem, I feel, is that I seem to develop a resentment of normal sexual relationships.' He had booked a room at the Savoy with the express intention of killing a prostitute: *any* prostitute; he had never met Catherine Russell before – had simply learnt that she was on the game, phoned her, agreed her price and fixed an appointment, and, a minute or so after her arrival, when she was getting ready, opened his knife and plunged it into her, and thereafter plunged it into her fifty-four times, at first frenziedly, then, when she was dead, with metronomic regularity, and then, towards the end of his mission, exhausted by it, as if in slow motion.

During the six months between his arrest at Southend and his trial at the Old Bailey, he was questioned, maybe more than once, by a psychiatrist, who concluded that he was suffering from 'a persistent psychopathic disorder leading to abnormally aggressive behaviour'. His counsel argued that as his, Marriott's, responsibility was diminished, he was guilty of manslaughter, not murder; the jury agreed; and the judge sent him to Broadmoor Hospital for the criminally insane 'without limitation of time'.

If his Legal Aid stretched to a subscription to a press-cutting agency, allowing him to see all of his notices, and to while away wet afternoons at Broadmoor by making a scrapbook, he must wish that he had chosen a different scene for his crime: Claridge's, Brown's, even the Arabic Dorchester – any hotel bar the Savoy would have been better in terms of himself-centred coverage. As it was, many reporters assigned to the second Savoy Killing gave less space to it, to him, than to reminders of the first Savoy Killing, done nearly sixty years before by a pretty Parisian called Marguerite Fahmy.

Hers was a hard act to follow.

Slaughter
at the Governor's Lodge

Chroniclers of crime (who, if they are at all good at the job, are basically novelists telling the truth) are vastly underprivileged compared with fictionists of crime. They cannot skirt a writer's block by, for instance, changing a method of murder in mid-scream, replacing a dull character with a quaint one, removing the scene of a crime from a semi-detached in Tooting to a five-star hotel in the West End, ironing out nonsenses in a plot, altering a murderer's licit occupation from that of butler to that of butcher for the simple reason that, as everyone knows by now, it is never the butler whodunnit. And they cannot – or rather, should not – have characters talking Capotely-precise prose or thinking *at all*. (The latter constraint means that the chronicler worth his salt is adrift from the cosy mooring that Ogden Nash termed *HIBK*, standing for *Had I But Known* – which, as Jacques Barzun and Wendell Hertig Taylor explain in their wonderful *A Catalogue of Crime* [New York, 1971], 'sums up the heroine's mind as she repeatedly ponders her failure to see the obvious traps laid for her by the villains, or as she recurrently regrets not having acted with ordinary judgment and spoken out in time, for reasons never stated to herself or the reader'; and it bars the chronicler from membership of what the book-dealing Jack Hammond of Ely calls the He-Must-Have School – e.g. 'As Tom Brown set about the grisly task of dismembering the late Mrs. Brown, his thoughts must have turned to their wedding-night'.)

And writers about *English* crimes suffer from the ordinariness of what most of the people concerned are called: the fictionist can tell his characters apart just by his christening of them (there is no chance of a novel-reader confusing the apparently blameless Loveinia Invernesshire with the plainly deceitful Hortense Garrotte, or the privately investigating Nick Sharp with the constabularian Aloysius Plodd) – but, nine times out of ten, the chronicler is stuck with Janes and Johns, such names preceding indiscriminately-distributed ones such as Brown, Jones, Patel, and Smith.

Writers about American crimes are better off – chiefly because natives of and settlers in that land tend to be ornately designated, but also because some American parents and priests and registrars of births go by drawled or mumbled sounds when spelling, and so add oddity to perfectly ordinary names (thus, an intended Barbara goes through life as Barbra, a Candice as Candace, a Deborah as Debra, a Jules as Yul, a Justin as Dustin); and even combinations that are drab by American standards – Oscar Hammerstein, for instance – are, if passed down, given uniqueness by the tagging on of sequential numbers, II, III, IV, and so on, till the latest in the line of parents, not knowing the Roman numeral that comes next, break the baptismal monotony.

An instance of the truth of the saying that, in the United States, clarity of characterisation begins at home is provided by what became known, maybe unfairly to a woman called Candace, as the Candy Murder Case.

Candace's husband, who played the non-speaking role of Victim in the affair, had originally been called Jakella Moscovitz, but long before becoming a dead millionaire thirty-three times over, had made his name as Jacques Mossler. Among others in the large cast were John V. Handwerker, who was the first of several doctors who looked at the corpse (he was not the pernickety one who counted thirty-nine stab-wounds in the torso and upper limbs and half a dozen blows to the head from a blunt instrument, and who made the neat observation that Mossler 'could have died from the stabbing, even if there had been no blows, and could have died from the blows if there had been no stabbing'); Melvin Lane Powers, the widow's favourite nephew; Earl C. Martin and Freddie Duhart, each of whom swore that Powers had offered him a fee to commit murder, the former saying that the offer was made – and turned down – a year or so prior to 30 June 1964, the date of Mossler's demise, and the latter saying that he received – and rejected – the offer only a month before that date; Billy Frank Mulvey, who stated that Candace Mossler had given him the first instalment of a payment for killing her husband but that he had welched on the deal, and Virgil Nelson Halford, who sought to cast doubt on Billy Frank's statement; Clyde Woody, senior spokesman for Candace when she and her nephew stood trial for her husband's murder; Nathan Greenbaum, Leroy P. Grigley and Clarence McQueen, members of an all-male and quarter-black jury that, because of peremptory challenges and challenges for cause by the aforementioned Mr. Woody and Melvin's leading counsel, the renowned though unimpressively-named Percy Foreman, took nine and a half days to amalgamate. The fact that three of the other nine jurors had surnames starting with Z – Zeller, Zellner and Zoller (making them sound to a reporter of the trial 'like Siamese Triplets') – indicates either that the queue of prospective jurors was in alphabetical order, and was just about gone by the time the jury was complete, or that Dade County, Florida, which was where both the murder and the trial took place, had more, far more, than its fair share of Z-initialled residents.

Candace's maiden-name was Weatherby. She was the sixth of a dozen children born to a small-time farmer and his wife, residing and toiling near the small town of Buchanan in the state of Georgia, just north of Florida. A record of her birth puts it in February 1920; but she, when grown up, insisted that she was not delivered till seven years later. If her insistence was justified, then she was a tender twelve when, in 1939, having been urged to marry a civil engineer named Johnson by one of her grandfathers, a bishop of the Mormon Church who had looked after her following the death of her mother and the decampment of her father, she did so. Whatever her age when she became Mrs. Johnson, her golden hair had grown long, her features were pretty in a pert sort of way, and her build, though small (perhaps because she had been stricken with polio; had for five years exercised her body to complete recovery), was pleasingly proportioned.

She gave birth to a son, called Norman, after his father, in 1943; to a daughter, called Rita, probably because Rita Hayworth was all the rage, a year later. Before Rita had mastered toddling, her father became ill; and her mother, forced to be the breadwinner, did a crash-course in dressmaking, then departed the family home for New York City, where she set up – and, it seems, prospered – as a fashion-designer. After but a year or so of designing, she turned to the task of being photographed for advertisements, and was soon specially in demand on behalf of dental products, for her front teeth, all her own, were immaculate. Her husband, well enough by now to have gone engineering in Canada, suggested a 'friendly divorce'; she having agreed, the formalities were completed; like it or not, she had custody of the children.

In 1949, when she was at least twenty-two, she moved to New Orleans, there to set up, all in one go, the Candace Finishing School, the Candace Modelling School, and the Candace Modelling Agency. In the first-named establishment, she tutored pupils towards becoming Southern (but not too Southern) Belles; in the second, graduates of the first were taught tricks of the modelling trade; the third hired out well-endowed alumni of the second for dressing and undressing assignments. Years later, reminiscing about her days down upon the Mississippi, she said:

'I was doing so well, I had time for art and culture. I volunteered to help raise money for the New Orleans Grand Opera Company. They gave me a list of businessmen to call on. Jacques Mossler, who had an office in New Orleans that year, was on my list.'

'*That year.*' Just one? Well, yes.

Indeed, only a few months of it. As an indirect result of the contribution-requesting call on Mr. Mossler, she became Mrs. Mossler before May was out. Having given some of his riches to her predecessor, he was 'down to four little finance companies'. He was fifty-four – and so thirty-two or twenty-five years older than Candace.

If what, when widowed, she said of the marriage night was true, Jacques had a faulty sense of time and place for revelations about himself that were liable to startle those in whom he confided. 'He told me . . . that women had made trouble for him – tried to blackmail him. To protect himself, he had undergone a sterilisation operation. He could never be victimised by a paternity suit.'

According to her recollections of post-nuptial discoveries concerning her husband's sexual inclinations, sterilisation had not impeded, may even have increased, his versatility. So far as I can tell, there was no corroboration of her allegations; but neither that nor the trial-judge stopped Percy Foreman, the loudest of the defenders she bought for her nephew, from declaring that, 'except for the shoe fetish, Mossler had 'em all – transvestite, homosexuality, voyeurism, masochism, sadism, all the perversions mentioned in *Psychopathia Sexualis*, Krafft-Ebing's great masterpiece'.

I may be showing my unsophistication by saying that the picture of Mossler as a Jacques of all errant traits is hard to reconcile with the seemingly firm fact that he was, nicely, a lover of children. When he divorced his first wife, the four daughters she had borne him were, at his legal pleading, allowed to stay with him; and one of his stipulations before marrying Candace was that his daughters and her Norman and Rita were to be treated as *their* children, equal recipients of their love and largesse. Wanting more children, but incapable of seeding any, he told Candace that they would adopt some – and amply fulfilled that intention in 1957, when a six-year-old girl and her three younger brothers were made waifs by the action of their father in shooting dead his wife and a still younger child, having mistaken them (so said psychiatrists who subsequently spoke up for him) for Japanese soldiers who had somehow missed the news that World War Two was over. The four children were added to the Mosslers' six, and Jacques straightway amended his will so as to ensure that each of the resultant ten would, when he died, receive no more, no less, than the others. As the diversification of his business interests – to include, as well as credit-finance houses, insurance companies and banks (called the Yes Banks – not to be confused with the British chain That Likes to Say Yes – because, according to advertisements, no one wanting a loan was ever turned down) – was making him pots of money, the children had the prospect of becoming fatherless or stepfatherless or foster-fatherless millionaires.

In case I have misled you into thinking that the children's ten-way split would account for Mossler's entire estate, I must explain that the arrangement applied only to part of what he would leave. His widow would be well provided for.

During the fifteen years before he was taken from her, he gave her, sexual requirements apart, everything she desired: jewels, flashy automobiles, bespoke clothes, an Egyptian maid who spoke three languages other than Egyptian, one, just as well, being English. There were other servants at her beck and call, some stationed in or around a 28-room house in the least undesirable part of Houston, Texas, that he bought for her, or on his present to her of a ranch south-east of Houston, just inland from the Gulf of Mexico, and some itinerant between the house and the ranch.

But for voluntary work in aid of a cause she considered worthy, she and Jacques would not have come together, and so it may be that he, not congenitally benevolent, was spurred by sentiment to put a little exertion and a lot of money behind her campaigns in support of cultural and social organisations (for instance, respectively, the Houston Grand Opera Association and a boys' club in the city) and of individuals who had fallen foul of the law.

It is hard to make out what attracted her to the cause of one person of the latter category, a disagreeable young man named Howard Stickney who had, perfectly properly, been sentenced to death for a specially barbaric double-murder. Not only were her efforts in vain (after thirteen stays of execution, all wholly or partly financed by Mossler, Stickney went to the electric chair), but as a result of them she met a man named Billy Frank Mulvey, a prison-mate of Stickney's, who, a few years later, when she herself stood in peril of legal extinguishment, did his best to point her towards that end.

More understandable than her espousal of Stickney's cause, when Johnny Will Ford, a black worker on her ranch, was sentenced to three years in prison for having habitually carried a concealed weapon, she took up the cudgels on his behalf, first of all arranging for his release on bond, and then talking the Governor of Texas into ordering his parole. Governor Daniel (his first name was Price – apt to the generality of politicians) was running for re-election. Those local newspapers that favoured one or other of his opponents were so vociferous in their condemnation of the clemency that he felt obliged to revoke the parole. While the police scoured Mossler property for the now-fugitive Ford (one officer, bespectacled, so irritated Candace by his insistence on peering in every nook and cranny that she gave him an upper-cut to the chin, sending his spectacles flying he knew not where, and so causing him to grope his way home, there to search for his contact-lenses), Governor Daniel issued press-statements that he, his advisers and theirs had been taken in by lies told by the parole-seeking Mosslers and their lawyers. Already upset by Daniel's reneging on a deal, Candace and Jacques were made revengeful by his besmirching of their reputations. They set about besmirching his, at the same time extolling virtues they perceived in one of his foes – contributing to his defeat by John Connally (who thereby acquired a mite of immortality, for it was he, proud Governor of the Lone Star State, who, seated in a car with, among others, President John F. Kennedy, was wounded by a bullet fired by Lee Harvey Oswald). Just prior to the poll, Johnny Will Ford surrendered to the police; when he was released from prison after serving a little of his sentence –

no time tacked on for the inconvenience he had caused by his disappearance – he went back to his job on the Mossler ranch.

Another of what Candace termed her 'fights for justice' was a family affair. A brother, DeWitt Weatherby, proprietor of a gambling establishment called the Silver Dollar Club in her native town of Buchanan, shot to death a regular customer, and, despite his explanation that he had acted self-defensively, was charged with murder. Candace rearranged her appointments so as to be free to attend the trial, but didn't seek to interfere with the legal process till (much to her surprise: thinking that acquittal was a foregone conclusion, she hadn't even offered to buy DeWitt top-notch defenders) her brother was found guilty and sentenced to life imprisonment. Thereupon, she collected Georgian lawyers much as poorer people collect Penny Blacks – at least fifty, it was reckoned by Governor Marvin Griffin, who was in the best position to keep count, since he was the target of their supplications. The trouble, from Candace's point of view, was that her collection was indiscriminate, including politico-lawyers who were not of Griffin's party: if he had granted the particular favour asked by them all, cronies and adversaries alike, the latter's cries of victory would have drowned out the former's tributes to his mercy. And so he refused to make DeWitt's durance briefer or less vile. 'But they got him out anyway,' Griffin subsequently grumbled, referring to the fact that DeWitt was released after serving only four years of his life sentence. Griffin's successor as governor was the lawyer who had worked hardest on behalf of DeWitt. Most of his electioneering expenses had been covered by Jacques Mossler.

Among others of Candace's kin to whom she gave succour was a nephew named Melvin Lane Powers, the son of one of her older sisters. He was born in 1941, which means that he was either twenty-one or fourteen years younger than his wealthy aunt. He was tall and well-built, and had jet-black hair, specially noticeable as eyebrows, a dishevelled nose, thick lips, and cheeks and a chin that, as well as being creased, were pitted with the scars of acne. He lacked social grace, and displayed an arrogance that he surely cannot have felt.

Candace doesn't seem to have paid much heed to her nephew till 1961 – though at some time during his late teens she may have gone out of her way to visit him: a subsequent business acquaintance of Melvin's recalled his saying 'that he was in jail in

Chicago – fraud for selling property or some stock or something, embezzlement, and that she [Candace] came to visit him or came to visit his cell-mate, and that's the way he got to know her'. Having been allowed to leave Chicago, Melvin hawked magazine subscriptions door-to-door in Arkansas on behalf of a company run by an ex-convict named Arthur Grimsley. Late in 1961, he forsook Mr. Grimsley and, after traipsing south-west, turned up at his aunt's house in Houston. She and her husband told him to make himself at home, which he did. Once he had put on weight, was chic in garments paid for by Candace, and was no longer able, credibly, to blame his sluggard behaviour on footsoreness, Jacques Mossler fabricated a job for him in one of his Houston-based finance companies.

About a year and a half later, Jacques came to the definite conclusion that Melvin had overstayed his welcome. Having imparted his conclusion to both Melvin and Candace, without receiving a co-operative response from either of them, he sacked Melvin and, since the latter still refused to find other accommodation, enlisted legal assistance in turfing him out of the house. Candace was most upset. Understandably so, in the view of those who, early in 1966, prosecuted her and her nephew on the charge of having murdered her husband: they believed that her distress at Melvin's eviction was occasioned by the fact that she had grown partial to incest.

According to one of the aforementioned prosecutors, Candace's distress was not prolonged. Shortly after the eviction of Melvin, Jacques travelled on his own to Europe, stayed abroad till the autumn of 1963, and then resided, not at the house in Houston, but in an apartment in Miami. The prosecutor:

'Upon moving to Miami, he lived over his office at Allen Parker Company, located on 36th Street. Powers and Candace remained in Houston. On 1 October 1963, Powers [who was now self-employed, trying, none too successfully, to sell caravans] rented an apartment and introduced Candace as his fiancée. She, Candace, would constantly visit the apartment, and witnesses saw them necking, kissing and hugging. Powers expressed to people how much he loved Candace, and that she was having marital complications and was in the process of obtaining a divorce, and that he, Powers, was going to marry her. On occasions Powers would refer to Candace Mossler as Miss Johnson, and on other occasions he even introduced Candace as his wife. Powers also told people that he loved her so much that he would kill for her.'

Earl C. Martin, one of the several witnesses for the prosecution who testified to having been approached by one or other of the defendants with offers of cash for the rendering of a lethal service, also swore that, on a date that he couldn't fix precisely – some time towards the end of 1963 – he, at Melvin's invitation, had listened in on an extension to a telephone conversation between Melvin and Candace, from which he had gathered that the former was keen on a pastime that he called 'eating pussy', and that the latter, possessor of the 'pussy', delighted in the former's 'eating' of it.

In the first week of June 1964, Candace, accompanied by her daughter Rita (on vacation from a university) and three of the adopted children (none older than thirteen), went to stay with Jacques, who had rented a small but luxurious apartment on the second floor (which in England would be termed the first) of a block called the Governor's Lodge, situated on Key Biscayne, a slight island close to Miami and connected to it by a stilted thoroughfare known as the Rickenbacker Causeway. The stay extended till the last day of the month, a Tuesday: early in the morning.

Early on three previous mornings, those of the 24th, 26th and 28th, Candace, complaining of migraine, had driven to the Jackson Memorial Hospital in Miami, there to beseech a palliative.

At about 1.30 a.m. on the 30th, she again drove to the mainland – this time (so she later told a policeman) not only because she felt a migraine coming on but also because she had some mail to post. She took the children with her.

That meant that her husband – who had celebrated his sixty-ninth birthday a few weeks before; had, at about the same time, been assured by his doctor that he was in tip-top condition – was left alone in the apartment. Alone, that is, apart from a recently-acquired dog, a boxer called Rocky after one or other of the so-known pugilists, Graziano and Marciano: a highly-strung beast, sparked into barking by the slightest sound that was uncommon.

One of the ubiquitous fictions of crime novels is that the time of a person's death can be established, give or take a minute or two, by feeling the warmth or otherwise of the skin, observing the extent and whereabouts of stiffening, peering at a thermometer that has been prodded into the rectum, and/or comparing stomach content with the last menu. The notion has been accepted as gospel by many lay readers of made-up crime tales – and, occasionally to the detriment of justice, by some people with medical diplomas. It is piffle.

Pleasingly, none of the doctors associated with what came to be called the Candy Murder Case needed to guess the time of Jacques Mossler's death.

For consider: shortly before 1.30, Mrs. Peggy Fletcher left her apartment across the corridor from Mossler's. She would be described by reporters as a 'socialite', which, considering that she worked as a typist for an insurance broker, suggests that that word has a less swell meaning in America than it has in England. One of the reporters would note that her dead-of-night emergence was so 'to keep from being caught short in the morning' – a further cause of confusion for English readers, to whom I must explain that she had run out of cigarettes. She went down to the parking lot and started her car, but found the exit blocked by Mossler's red Pontiac convertible, which she noticed contained all but Candace of the visiting members of his family. As soon as the Pontiac had been obligingly reversed by Rita, Mrs. Fletcher drove to a shop that she thought would be open but which was not. When she returned, still cigaretteless, to the Governor's Lodge, there was no sign of the Pontiac.

She went up to her apartment, undressed, and got into bed – and had been there 'perhaps five minutes' when she was disturbed by the barking of a dog. Then: 'I heard the sounds of a scuffle. There was a distinct thud, and someone cried out, "Don't do this to me!" I heard another thud. The dog continued to bark. Then I heard footsteps running down the corridor – heavy footsteps. Without a doubt, it was a man.'

The barking had awoken Herbert House, tenant of the apartment directly above Mossler's. It was not the first time that he had been annoyed by the noisiness of Rocky; over the past few weeks, he had complained to Mossler and to a manager of the Governor's Lodge. Now he switched on the bedside lamp and, thinking to get exact data for a letter of furious complaint, looked at his watch. *1.45.* House got out of bed, scampered across to the balcony, and, looking down, saw that the abominable Rocky was skittering about on Mossler's balcony, impounded there by the closed glass doors of the apartment. 'I heard those sliding doors open, and I called down to ask if they were going to take the dog in. I heard a voice answer, "Yeah." It seemed to be the voice of a young man.' House went back to bed and straightway fell into a sleep of such soundness that, despite forthcoming noises, he did not stir till his accustomed breakfast-time.

One may assume that House had only just returned to the Land of Nod when Mrs. Irene Durr, night-manager of the building, was awoken in her first-floor apartment by a scream. Sitting up in bed and switching on the light, she heard barks – which cued drowsy surmise that Rocky had nipped its master, causing him, first, to scream, then to retaliate, causing Rocky, in turn, to raise a rumpus. Before turning off the light and settling down again, she looked at her watch and saw that it registered 1.30. (A subsequent checking of the watch showed that it was fifteen minutes slow.)

No sooner had she settled down than she heard running footsteps on the stairs. Deciding that she had better do some night-managing, she arose and stepped into the lobby, just in time to espy someone leaving the building by the back door. Through the glass panel in that door, she could see an area of the parking lot: the area reserved for Mr. Mossler's vehicles. 'The person went to a white Chevrolet in the lot. The walk didn't seem like a woman. The person got in the Chevrolet and drove off.' (The apparent uniformity of American cars to English eyes makes it surprising to Englishmen that Americans are so good at telling one make from others: it seems as ophthalmically acute as finding a needle in a haystack and, without reliance on a law of probability, declaring that the needle found is the needle that was sought.)

A moment before Mrs. Durr had stepped into the lobby, a home-coming tenant, Martin Tavel, manager of a Miami radio station, had entered the lobby by the front door, and so he got a longer look at the person hurrying out at the back than did Mrs. Durr. He would tell the police that the person was definitely a man – a tall man whose dark hair was so long that no skin was visible between it and the collar of his dark shirt.

Tavel and Mrs. Durr walked out of the front door. The white Chevrolet was coming round the corner of the building, its headlamps on. As the car came closer, the lamps were switched off: only for a few seconds, though: the lamps came on again before the car turned into the street and sped in the direction of the Rickenbacker Causeway.

Rocky's barking caused Tavel to look up, to notice that lights were on in Jacques Mossler's apartment. He and Mrs. Durr took the elevator to the second floor. As they emerged into the corridor, so did Peggy Fletcher. The three became a whispering trio by the door of Jacques Mossler's apartment, and then Mrs. Fletcher, who loved dogs, even Rocky, and seems to have had a way with them, cooed through the keyhole till the boxer was lulled into silence. Pleasure at the peacefulness taking over from interest in what had excited the dog, the three retired to their respective beds. The time was close to two o'clock.

By then, presumably, Candace and her charges were in Miami – a city that was still safe to visit, even in the small hours: not yet ineradicably contaminated by people whose migration from Cuba made that island a nicer place. The pain in Candace's head cannot have been severe, for after buying stamps and posting whatever she stuck them on, she escorted her children to a public lounge in the DuPont Plaza Hotel, tarried with them there until about four o'clock, and only then made her way to the emergency room in the Jackson Memorial Hospital for her regular, alternate-nights dose of a balm that she must have considered more potent than anything available from an all-night chemist.

She left the hospital at five minutes past four. That time is of less interest than the reason for its being known. Only a moment after she had gone, Maida Loretta Kolodgy, the clerk in the emergency room, took a telephone call from a man wanting to speak to Mrs. Mossler – the same man, Ms Kolodgy felt sure, who had called twice before, making a similar request, during the past hour and twenty minutes. Ms Kolodgy looked outside; but, returning to the telephone, told the caller that there was no sign of Mrs. Mossler.

Who was the man? Why was he so keen to speak to Candace? And – most intriguing of all – what gave him the idea that she might be reached at the hospital? After all, unless the regularity of her previous attacks of migraine had forewarned her that another was imminent, and she spoke of what was to come, how she would deal with it, to a male acquaintance prior to about one o'clock, when – so she subsequently said – she experienced the first twinges, her husband seems to have been the only man who could have known that she was going to Miami and that the hospital was one of her destinations there. Of course, the man may have telephoned or called at the apartment soon after her departure and learned of her proposed hospital visit from Jacques.

For various reasons, none of the questions was provided with a sure answer. Jacques could not help. Candace expressed mystification. The caller never revealed himself.

4.30 or thereabouts. Mrs. Durr, roused by the sound of a car pulling up in the parking lot, and made wide-awake by the patter of five pairs of feet in the lobby, turned on the light and looked at her unreliable watch.

4.45 Dr. John V. Handwerker, a physician of Key Biscayne, heard from an answering-service girl that Rita Mossler had requested his presence at the Mossler apartment, where there had been 'trouble – maybe a killing'. He told the girl to ring the police, then dressed and drove to the Governor's Lodge.

4.29 James Jorgenson, a young deputy sheriff who had recently applied for leave of absence so that he might study criminology at the Florida State University, knocked on the door of the apartment and was admitted by Candace, who told him, 'He's over there,' indicating a yellow-blanketed mound in a corner of the living room. Noticing much blood as he crossed the room, Jorgenson tried to prepare himself against horror when he lifted the blanket. It was as well for him that he did so, for the sight of the stabbed and battered body of Jacques Mossler, clad only in a once-white undershirt, would shock and sicken even those subsequently-arriving older officers who believed that their emotions had been used up. (At the trial, the judge refused to let the jury see photographs of the body, saying that they were 'inflammatory'.) Remembering that he was duty-bound to put his fingers where there had once been a pulse, Jorgenson touched below the right ankle, one of the few unbloodied parts of the body, before replacing the blanket. Then he telephoned his headquarters. He observed that 'the room did not appear to be ransacked. There was a large dog in the kitchen. Rita and one of the children took the dog into one of the bedrooms.'

4.53 Dr. Handwerker arrived. In terms of handiwork, he did no more than confirm Jorgenson's conviction that Mr. Mossler was dead. But he observed the widow, wondering, without coming to a conclusion, whether or not she was in clinical shock. She was dry-eyed. 'She kept herding the children in and out.'

An hour or so passed. It would be nice to know what happened in the apartment meanwhile, but neither Jorgenson nor Handwerker seems to have considered any incidents worthy of mention. In England, someone would have made tea; but the result of a later examination of work-surfaces in the kitchen indicates that nobody made a hot beverage of any kind. The thought that someone may have passed round cans of a fizzy drink is too distasteful to contemplate.

6.10 – and all of a sudden the already crowded apartment became claustrophobic, with the advent of two members of the homicide division of the local constabulary, several scene-of-crime officers, laden with apparatus, and the medical examiner for Dade County.

One of the homicide detectives, Lieutenant Jerry Evans, cleared a bedroom of occupants, then invited Candace and Rita into it for a talk. He asked Candace if she had any idea who might have committed the murder, and she replied that her husband – a ruthless, at times vicious businessman – must have made many enemies, adding that a used-car dealer in Miami, whom she named, had a severe grievance against him. She went on to say that she believed that the apartment had been ransacked. When asked if she had any grounds for the belief, she pointed at two unzipped hold-alls in a closet in the bedroom; also she said that her husband's wallet was empty of cash, that some of her jewellery was missing, and that two hundred-dollar bills that she had left in the bathroom were gone.

Enquiring about the jaunt to Miami, Lieutenant Evans mentioned that he had had a few words with Peggy Fletcher. She had told him, he said, that when she had left the building at 1.30, intending to buy cigarettes, she had seen the four Mossler children sitting in a red Pontiac – but not their mother.

Rita explained that Candace had just popped back to the apartment to pick up something that she had forgotten. Evans asked Candace to amplify her daughter's recollection, but received what he later called a 'noncommittal answer'.

Evans, who seems to have been a most unassertive detective, requested Candace's presence at the sheriff's office later that morning. She arrived on time, chaperoned by a lawyer, and made a brief formal statement in which, perhaps unintentionally, she added a possible motive for the murder to those which she had earlier supported or suggested. The new possibility (which would, never mind its lack of corroboration, entrance the legal defenders of Candace and Melvin) was that Jacques Mossler, having turned to homosexuality, had been slain by one of his own male lovers whom he had slighted, disappointed or something of that frenzy-encouraging sort, or by the lover of one of them, wanting to eradicate competition. Evans paraphrased the relevant part of Candace's statement as follows: 'She told me that she felt her husband had boyfriends. She said he had received calls from Texas from a male voice that had feminine tones.'

As Candace and her lawyer were leaving, Evans asked her for details of the jewellery that she had told him was missing from the apartment, and she promised to send him a list. During the two following days, he telephoned Candace nine times, and Rita five, invariably pleading for the list, but never did get it. After Candace's departure from the sheriff's office, he had no direct contact with her. Until the trial, his only glimpse of her was over the heads of reporters and cameramen, outside the premises of an undertaker who had arranged for her husband's body to be shipped to Washington, D.C., for burial in the Arlington National Cemetery.

By then, other officers of the law – some far-flung from Florida – were getting quite excited over what one of them was audacious enough to describe as 'evidential developments of an incremental nature that are confidently expected to nail the Mossler malefactor – singular or plural'.

The knife that was used to inflict thirty-nine wounds in Jacques Mossler's body was never identified. The blunt instrument that was used to bludgeon him may have been either an empty soft-drink bottle, found in the kitchen by a scene-of-crime officer, or a heavy glass swan, one of a pair in the apartment, that was lying in pieces on the living-room carpet, the head and neck of it so close to the body that what would otherwise have been a puddle of blood was turned into two serpentine streams.

Of all the surfaces in the apartment that were examined for fingerprints, the most immaculate was a Formica-covered counter that abutted the kitchen-sink. It had been scrubbed by Roscoe Brown, a black servant of Mossler's, during the afternoon preceding the murder. The scene-of-crime officers found only one blemish on it: the print of the palm of a hand. In every particular, the print matched that of the palm of one of Melvin Lane Powers' hands.

The search for the white Chevrolet seen by Irene Durr and Martin Tavel took investigators to the Miami offices of the Allen Parker Company, the agency used by Mossler for his credit-financing activities in southern Florida. There they learned that on 23 June, a week before the crime, Candace had asked to borrow any one of the cars repossessed by the company from clients who had fallen far behind with repayments. A four-year-old white Chevrolet having been picked out, it was, at her request, delivered to her at the Miami International Airport. The deliverer – who also handed over $125 that she had asked the company manager for – was the already-mentioned Roscoe Brown. He had been employed by Jacques Mossler for seventeen years, and was so grateful for the employment that he had had his son christened Roscoe Mossler Brown. Candace gave him a lift back to within a block of the Parker offices, then went on to some unknown destination with her other passenger, who had been waiting with her at the airport. Roscoe was loathe to identify that person to the police, but eventually succumbed to their blandishments and said that it was Melvin Lane Powers.

The Parker Company's records showed that the borrowed car had not been returned. Rather than ask Candace if she knew where it was, the investigators at once circulated a description of it among their own and neighbouring organisations. It was soon noticed, parked a yard or so away from the police station at the airport. The doors were unlocked. The keys were resting on a sun-visor. And so was a parking slip, dispensed by a machine at the entrance to the lot: the slip had been stamped at 5.19 on the morning of 30 June – about three and a half hours after someone had driven, if not this car, then one very much like it, away from the Governor's Lodge on Key Biscayne. The car was towed to a garage, and there examined – presumably for transferred bloodstains as well as for fingerprints. None of the former was found, but there was an extravagance of the latter, including nineteen belonging to Melvin Lane Powers.

The police amassed documentary and eye-witness evidence that Powers had flown from Houston to Miami (a distance of almost a thousand miles, east-south-east) on the afternoon of Monday, 29 June, arriving shortly before six o'clock. Similarly, that he had made the return trip the following day, leaving Miami after nine o'clock in the morning.

Information regarding Powers' whereabouts during the hours between his arrival from Houston and the murder was fragmentary. It seems that the only persons who subsequently recalled seeing him were Badar Shehan and Marshall Klein, respectively a bartender in and the manager of the Stuft Shirt Lounge of the Holiday Inn at the Miami end of the Rickenbacker Causeway. According to Shehan, he served Powers with a drink between half-past six and seven on the Monday evening; Powers asked for and was provided with an empty soft-drink bottle, but did not take it with him when he left. According to Klein, Powers returned a few minutes later, saying that he had forgotten to take the empty bottle, was given it or another, and walked out. According to Shehan, Powers reappeared just before the closing time of one o'clock, ordered and paid for a double Scotch, quickly downed it, and left.

Paul Peter O'Neill, Powers' only full-time employee at his caravan-sales establishment near Houston, said that when Powers left for the airport on the 29th, he was wearing dark clothes, but that when he returned next day he was wearing clothes of a light colour, the trousers so inadequate to his inside-leg measurement that they barely overlapped his socks. (Months after the murder, a dark jacket and pair of trousers, both stained with blood, were found by police in the Mosslers' Houston house; an eye-witness to Powers' presence at Miami airport on the morning of the 30th was shown the garments, and stated, apparently without hesitation, that they were those he had seen Powers wearing.)

Several persons swore that, during the period between Powers' eviction and firing by Jacques Mossler and the latter's sudden death, they had, each apart from the others, had conversations with Powers or with his aunt, or with both, in the course of which they had been sounded as to whether, if the price was right, they would commit a contract-killing; and one of those persons, Billy Frank Mulvey, went so far as to say that Candace had given him an advance payment towards a fee agreed between them for his murder of her husband, but that he had simply grabbed the money and run.

Not all of the above-outlined evidence had been garnered by the

dame Fahmy.

Prince Ali Kamel Fahmy Bey.

artoon reproduced from
ro's comic weekly Kachkoul,
icting Ali Fahmy (right), his
etary, and his secretary's
etary. It appeared above these
ds: 'The Light, the Shadow of
Light, and the Shadow of the
dow of the Light.'

The Fahmys on their honeymoon
at Luxor.

A room in a Savoy suite such as the Fahmys would have taken.

Sir Edward Marshall Hall.   *Mr. Justice Swift.*

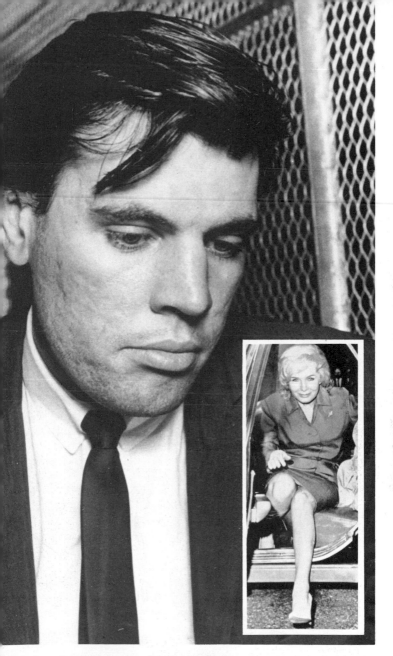

Melvin Lane Powers. Candace Mossler (insert).

Lord and Lady Lucan.

The Lucans' house,
Lower Belgrave Street, London.

The nanny, Sandra Rivett.

Baron Erich von Schauroth.

The Castle at Blinkoog.

Colleen and Dieter.

The Beretta, with bullets and cartridge cases.

Michael Telling.

Lambourne House.

police by 3 July. But by that date they believed they had sufficient evidence to justify their arrest of Melvin Lane Powers.

His aunt heard of his detention within hours of its beginning – as soon as she disembarked at Houston airport from the aeroplane that had brought her from Washington, D.C., where she had been chief mourner at a funeral. The news was screamed at her – obliquely, in the form of personal questions – by a foregathered pack of reporters. Ignoring the impertinence, she trotted to a limousine and was sped to her home. There, she straightway made her best efforts to ensure Melvin's protection. It may have crossed her mind that by protecting him, she was also protecting herself.

The suspicion that that was so would inspire an anonymous versifier to compose a couplet:

> *Candy is dandy;*
> *But, for mercy, yells: 'Percy!'*

The surname of the Percy to whom Candace yelled was Foreman. He was a Texan defence-lawyer, skilled at, among other things, recognising intelligent prospective jurors, ensuring that few of them served, and concentrating the minds of those he allowed into the jury-box on irrelevancies and side-issues. That he didn't give a cuss for justice seems to be indicated by his statement: 'You should never allow the defendant to be tried. Try someone else – the husband, the lover, the police, or, if the case has social implications, society generally. But never the defendant.' And that he believed that he was worth every penny of his fees, which were among the highest in the land, is shown by his comment: 'It's not that I'm vain, proud or egotistical. I just don't have anything to be modest about.'

His asking price for looking after Melvin was $200,000. Candace guarenteed part of that amount by handing over to Foreman the choicest items in her recently-depleted collection of jewellery, and signing a document saying that he could sell all of them if his bill was not met within a week. Then she upped and went to Rochester, Minnesota, where, having booked sessions with a specialist on migraine at the Mayo Clinic, she rented two apartments, one for herself, the other in which her adopted children could squeal to their hearts' content without exacerbating pains in her head.

Foreman's first action towards earning his fee was to apprise press and television news editors that, once their representatives were outside the jail in which his client was incarcerated, he would be there too, blustering newsworthily. Having performed, he threatened the jailers with all sorts of dire consequences if they were foolish enough to argue against his interpretation of his and Melvin's rights, and then spoke privately with Melvin, saliently for the purpose of ordering him not to say anything to anyone unless he, Foreman, had rehearsed him in an utterance and told him when to utter it.

For almost a year, Foreman resisted efforts by the Floridan authorities to have Powers extradited from Houston to Miami. Meanwhile, the police strengthened their case against both Powers and Candace – and she, acting on her own initiative or in response to suggestions from paid advisers, sought to diminish the police case and to lend apparent substance to her assertion that her late husband was homosexual.

Hearing that Roscoe Brown had made an additional statement – to the effect that the white Chevrolet she had borrowed had been in the parking lot at the Governor's Lodge in the afternoon prior to the murder – she wrote to the faithful retainer, asking him to telephone her, reversing the charge. Roscoe obeyed. He had two long conversations with Candace, during which she did her utmost to persuade him to retract his statements. Every word of the conversations was tape-recorded by the police.

She actually did persuade a man named William Measamer, who worked at the Houston branch of the Allen Parker Company, to swear that Jacques Mossler was homosexual. Soon afterwards, however, Measamer suddenly suffered a severe attack of cold feet, probably a side-effect of a district attorney's dissertation to him on the penalties for perjury, and declared on his oath that, so far as he knew, Mossler was as heterosexual as the day was long, and that he would never have said otherwise had not Candace, generous to him to a fault, pleaded with him to do so on a number of occasions, most urgently when they were in bed together in her apartment in Rochester.

On 20 July 1965, in Miami, a grand jury returned an indictment of murder in the first degree against Melvin Lane Powers and Candace Mossler. Melvin had recently settled in at a local jail. Candace, having surrendered voluntarily, was escorted to another. Percy Foreman, retained by her to represent Melvin, conferred with lawyers she had retained for herself, and it was agreed that though he and they should give the appearance of being separate forces, they would regard him as the chief defence lawyer. The Foreman Alliance soon scored a spectacular success, by getting the prisoners released on bail of $50,000 each.

On 17 January 1966, the trial proceedings at last began. It took the lawyers till the last day of that month to gather twelve jurors and three reserves. The forensic farce was made more farcical by the judge's decision that, as neither defendant was in custody, it would be unfair on the jurors if he were to stick to the convention that jurors in such a case should be kept to themselves, night and day, for the duration of the trial; his admonition to them that, while their time was their own, they were not to read press accounts of the case, listen to radio broadcasts about it, or watch items on it in televised news programmes, seems to have passed unheeded, going by the fact that on the morning after a newspaper report referred to their general lack of sartorial elegance, each and every one of them turned up in his Sunday-best.

The trial, which rambled on until Sunday, 6 March, brought disgrace upon the American legal profession. But, perhaps because so many members of that profession had already brought disgrace upon it, no one expressed much concern. Throughout the trial, lawyers on both sides, prosecution and defence, knowingly broke the most elementary rules: every few minutes, a lawyer said something that he knew perfectly well he had no right to say, an opponent objected, and the judge ordered the offending words stricken from the record – adding, ridiculously, that the jury was to ignore them. Perhaps the most blatant instance of a 'professional foul' was when Percy Foreman, wanting to discredit a prosecution witness, spoke loudly to himself, wondering whether or not the judge would allow him to introduce evidence pertaining to the witness's criminal record. (Having used the sporting term 'professional foul', let me suggest to Americans who feel that the Law should have something to do with Justice that they might campaign for judges to be given one of the powers of football referees: a forensic equivalent of a Yellow Card would be shown to a persistent offender, who if he fouled thereafter, would be shown a Red Card, indicating a set period of debarment from advocacy, starting as soon as the current trial was over.)

The prosecution lawyers seem to have been so intent on

thinking up ways in which they themselves could cheat and on listening for objectionable remarks from the defenders that they quite failed to notice any of the umpteen illogicalities that Foreman & Có. fed to the jury. The most glaring of these concerned the solitary palm-print, undoubtedly Melvin's, found on the sink-side counter in the kitchen of the apartment at the Governor's Lodge. Ignoring the fact that the print showed – unequivocally, if Roscoe Brown's evidence as to his charring was accepted – that Melvin was in the apartment within hours of its becoming the scene of a crime, Foreman contended that since some of the prints found on comparatively grubby surfaces in the apartment had not been identified, one or several of them might have been deposited by the 'true culprit': ergo, Melvin's (timed) print was no more suspicious than any of the unattributed ones.

Needless to say, neither defendant ventured to the witness-stand.

The jury took sixteen and a half hours, spread over two and a half days, to agree on the verdicts; they spent the nights at an hotel where one of them normally worked as a bell-hop.

The judge, whose name was Schulz, seemed to be surprised by what he read on the verdict-recording slips passed to him, via a bailiff, by the foreman of the jury. He told the clerk of the court to read the verdicts aloud. Melvin uttered one word – 'Beautiful' – when he heard that he had been found not guilty. And Candace, knowing that her nephew's acquittal meant that she was free as well, started sobbing with relief before the clerk read from the other slip.

Some months after the trial, Candace and Melvin announced that they were engaged to be married. Nothing came of it, however. Early in 1969, Candace took Melvin to court, accusing him of having beaten her up after ordering her to 'stay home where I belonged'. She subsequently married a tall Texan.

She and Melvin stuck together in one respect. They fought a long-running battle with Percy Foreman over his bill, saying that the collateral that each of them had put up (jewellery from her, a land-deed from him) had not only been misappropriated but, what with inflation, had grown in value, putting the lawyer in their debt. Foreman countered: 'Mrs. Mossler would not have inherited one penny had she not been acquitted. I was charged with the ultimate responsibility of seeing that both clients were successfully defended against the murder charges. Lawyers often work on a fifty-fifty contingency-fee basis. Therefore, I feel I have a fifty-percent interest in whatever amount Mrs. Mossler profited by the acquittal. I will settle for any reasonable amount between 4.5 million dollars and 16.5 million dollars.' Later, he said that he hoped that the argument would be aired in court: 'As an outcome of such a trial and evaluation of my services, the public might have a better opinion than it now has as to who killed Jacques Mossler.' How the argument was resolved, if it ever was, doesn't appear to have been reported.

I think that Candace should have the last word. When a journalist reminded her of some of the terrible things that had been said about her, and asked if she wished to comment, her reply was: 'Well, sir, nobody's perfect.'

The Imperfect
English Gentleman

The remark about a Scots thane of the eleventh century, 'Nothing in his life Became him like the leaving of it,' can be applied, with more certitude, to an English lord of the twentieth. Following his remove in November 1974, the press, keen to find something good to say about him, offered the majority of his few non-gambling, incidentally decent, acquaintances recompense for said quote, but tempted no more than a couple to perjure themselves. One of his gambling cronies, not paid to speak, made others of his kind snigger by declaiming, 'He was a warrior, a Roman,' and adding, 'He was quite capable of falling on his sword, so to say.' A sniggerer remarked: 'He was also quite capable of shooting himself in the foot, so to say.'

As at the time of the disappearance of Dr. Crippen, and of the quest for Mr. Qualtrough during the Wallace murder case, a sly rhymester found a sort of inspiration in Baroness Orczy's Scarlet Pimpernel lines:

> They seek him here, they seek him there –
> The fuzz, they seek him everywhere.
> They haven't found a single clue yet
> To the whereabouts of Lord Lucan of Roulette.

> If he's not in Heaven or Hell,
> One thing's sure – his pals won't tell:
> His arrest, to them, would be bad news,
> Unless he had paid his IOUs.

Richard John Bingham was born in December 1934, the first son of parents who would, fifteen years later, become the sixth Earl and the Countess of Lucan. His great-great-grandfather was that Lord Lucan who, with insufficient concern for the consequences, ordered the Light Brigade to charge during the battle of Balaclava.

Child psychologising is quite as unreliable as the grown-up kind, but it does seem likely that his early years were confused by his parents' selective socialism, exemplified by the fact that, while they both railed against inherited privileges and spoke longingly of a British Meritocracy (the mother was secretary of the St. John's Wood Labour Party, the father became the Labour Whip in the House of Lords), they sent him to Eton. Jonathan Miller, a contemporary of his at that school, has said that the mother 'was always wielding Labour Party pamphlets. She did look a sight in a rather impressive way that would probably have shocked only the parvenus. It would probably have been more shocking at Radley than at Eton. Her hair was a wonderful mess, as if someone had stabbed a sofa.'

Straight after leaving Eton, Bingham was conscripted for National Service. He became an officer in the Coldstream Guards, his father's old regiment. He looked fine in uniform, specially when his moustache had grown full, but impressed no one by his soldiering. Still, he made something of a name for himself from his off-duty pastimes – indoors, as an untiring player of contract-bridge; outdoors, as a bob-sleigher, so casual about the risks that he was made a member of the Army team.

Demobilised, he joined the merchant bankers, William Brandt & Co., in the City of London, as a management trainee, his starting salary being £500 a year. A fellow-trainee afterwards said of him: 'His intelligence may not have been too bad, but as far as education was concerned, he was a very limited fellow. Even in those days his horizons stopped at Jules Bar.' The latter comment is too hard on him. In fact, he spent comparatively little of his spare time at the just-mentioned bar in Jermyn Street; or at any bar, for that matter. Usually, he gambled.

In 1960, so the story goes, he won £20,000 at a session of *chemin de fer*, and at once forsook merchant banking for full-time gambling. If the date is correct, then his timing was opportune, for it was in that year that the Betting and Gaming Act was passed, legalising the playing of games of chance for money. According to another professional gambler, his years at Brandt's had taught him to be 'a good money manager' – which was as well, because he was rated only reasonably adept at poker, and no better than average at bridge and the variant on ludo called backgammon. No doubt he would have felt impelled to frequent the Clermont Club in

Berkeley Square, just along from the Maggs Brothers' bookshop, but the owner of the place, thinking of him as 'good furniture', likely to attract impressionable wealthy punters, gave him an incentive to play there by doubling his stakes when they became too high for him.

He played a six-day week, and the weeks were almost as unvaried as his costume: each suit he bought was a dark, pin-striped replica of the one he had bought before; he needed to be coaxed to speak to persons who didn't have shoelaces as 'proper' as his own (not that he had much to say to anybody – particularly not during a game, when, in the opinion of one opponent, his poker-face was less indicative of control than of blankness). His days began about noon, with vodka-martinis at the St. James's Club; then he took a cab to the Clermont for lunch – always smoked salmon and lamb cutlets, the latter *en gelée* in the summer – followed by gambling till six or so, when he went home to spruce himself up; after dinner (every Friday, virtually without fail, at the Mirabelle in Curzon Street) he gambled again, on Mondays and Thursdays starting off with bridge at the then nomadic Portland Club, continuing till the small hours, usually at the Clermont.

He rarely broke his routine so as to indulge in 'boffing' (Sloane-Rangerese at that time for sex). One of the Clermont crowd thought that 'he saw women as an inferior race. He was often embarrassed in their company. If anything, I would say that he would perform only the occasional *boff de politesse*.'

And so, in November 1963, there were ripples of surprise in gaming-clubland from his marriage, at the Holy Trinity church near Harrods, to Veronica Duncan, who was five years younger than himself, and whom he had first met at the start of 1963, when she was a bridesmaid at her sister's wedding, in the same church, to his friend William Shand-Kydd, whose family was wealthy from wallpaper. The surprise was tinged with shock at the fact that Veronica was a commoner – that disadvantage not overcome by prosperity. Her father, a regular officer in the army, had been killed in a car-crash when she was two and her sister was not yet born; the depleted family had moved from Uckfield, Sussex, to Bournemouth, and then away to South Africa, where the widow had met and married a man named Margrie, once a navigator in the RAF, who had brought her and her daughters back to England, and become landlord of the Wheatsheaf at North Waltham, near

Basingstoke – a hostelry dismissed by Egon Ronay but known to one member of the Clermont as 'a pub on the way back from Ascot'.

Why, it wasn't as if Veronica had oodles going for her in the way of looks: she had once been a model, but only for teenage clothes, which fitted her slight figure becomingly. Not the sort of gel most Clermont chaps would have been eager to boff.

A bit of a puzzle, too. She made it clear, right from the start of her marriage, that she found gambling a bore – yet, night after night, she turned up at the Clermont and sat with other wives but aloof from them, smoking quite heavily, drinking hardly at all, taking no apparent interest in whether her husband was winning or losing, until, well before midnight, she indicated to him that she was leaving, and left. The other wives couldn't make her out – couldn't, for instance, decide whether she was being starry-eyed or sarcastic when, enveigled into speaking of her marriage, she referred to it as her 'elevation'.

Two months after the wedding, she was further elevated, to the rank of countess. That came about through her father-in-law's death; her husband's succession to the title of seventh Earl of Lucan.

An inheritance came with the title. There was, inter alia, the family silver; there was income from land in England ('considerable' acreage on the northern side of the Thames, near Staines, and, just across the river, 100 acres that were leased by a golf club – of which Lucan automatically became president) and land and property in Ireland (chiefly in and around Castlebar, the capital of County Mayo, where more than 600 tenants were supposed to pay ground-rent to a Lucan family trust). The trouble, from the new earl's point of view, was that only a modicum of what went into various trust funds was doled out to him – about £10,000 a year, if the reckoning he mentioned to friends was true. I cannot make out whether or not that amount included interest-payments on money deposited in his name in banks in Switzerland, the Bahamas, and what was then called Rhodesia. The Bank of England was enforcing exchange-control, and so – officially, at any rate – he could only withdraw and spend money from the overseas accounts when he was abroad.

Perhaps it was because of that stricture that, during the first few summers of his married life, he often travelled to the gambling centres of Europe, taking Veronica with him. Being xenophobic, he did not enjoy the jaunts. According to one acquaintance, if Lucan had ever spoken in the House of Lords, it would have been in a debate on immigration: 'He felt very strongly about that. You see, Lucan came from a family who in their origins were the old clan-leaders of the Anglo-Saxons, and I think he felt a great worry for what he saw as the hybridisation and miscegenation of the island-race. A lot of people in a bus queue in Nuneaton might feel the same, but then it's not their responsibility.' And another acquaintance said of him that 'his basic attitude was that wogs begin at Calais – he hated "abroad"'. Ten years or so after the trips, Veronica would refer to them as 'always business,' adding: 'In Monte Carlo and Gstaad I was really a "front". We looked like a happy holiday couple together, but he was really there for the big games. In Monte Carlo it was backgammon on the beach during the day and the casino at night. In Gstaad it was backgammon with the Greeks.'

Soon after becoming the Countess of Lucan, Veronica became pregnant. And, about the same time, her husband (who had already been nicknamed, at first unpleasingly to him, 'Lucky Lucan') paid £19,000 for a tall house, five floors over a basement, on the south-eastern, least desirable edge of Belgravia: about twice as far from Hyde Park Corner, to the north, as from Victoria Station, to the south, and with a glimpse of Buckingham Palace through the rear windows, facing east, on the top floor. The house was at the top end of Lower Belgrave Street, the first south of Eaton Square: No. 46. A hundred yards down the street, on the same side, were a few places of trade – first, a baker's, then (handy for Veronica, whenever she ran out of cigarettes) a small, single-bar pub called The Plumbers' Arms, decorated in browns, lit salmon-pink at night, and then the premises of John Lidstone, butcher by appointment to both the Queen and the Queen Mother.

Lucan left the furbishment of the house to Veronica, apart from insisting that wall-space was to be found for every one of the framed portraits of his ancestors (pride of place went to a painting of the third Earl, which was hung at the centre of a wall in the dining room, opposite a painting of the ginger-whiskered Lord Cardigan, leader of the charge of the Light Brigade), and that a small room off the first landing was to be his sanctum sanctorum, lined with shelves for inherited leather-bound volumes and for books that he had bought or would buy (nearly all crime novels, biographies of tycoons, manuals on the games that he played for a living), crammed with evidences that he was a gambler (for instance, a gate-leg card-table, a cabinet filled with ivory chips – an engagement-present, that, bought for him by Veronica, frightfully extravagantly, from Asprey's in New Bond Street), and with, additional to a desk and chair, a coffee-table whose sole purpose was to keep off the floor the box containing his robes of scarlet and ermine (which would be unfolded and shaken free of tissue-paper just once each year, for his only visits to the House of Lords, on days when the Queen opened Parliament).

The Lucans' first child, a girl whom they called Frances, was born in October 1964. A son, Lord George Bingham, heir to the Lucan title, was born in 1967, and a second daughter, Camilla, three years later. Each, when small, was looked after by female workers temporarily calling themselves nannies – some in their teens, none trained for the job, and only one sticking at it for long. There was no single reason for the brisk turnover: one or two of the nannies were sacked by Veronica on account of their incompetence or laziness; a few, opportunistic au-pairs, left the Lucans in the lurch once they had found more comfortable, better paid employment or had been offered accommodation in boyfriends' residences. And three, at least, walked out in reaction to the moodiness of the mistress of the house.

Certainly, Veronica was prone to depression. That was so before her marriage; more so afterwards – increasingly so after she had given birth to a son. Then, perhaps because she felt that her heir-producing labours had left her useless so far as her husband was concerned, she became almost a recluse: usually idle as well as lonely, hobby-less if her infrequent dabbing of paint on canvas is disregarded; she sneered at the *Tatler*-extolled charity-work done by other 'Clermont grass-widows', saying that it was a kind of occupational therapy.

The Lucans' married life was no life at all: not for either of them. It is surprising that they stayed together – or rather, continued to share an address – for more than nine years. They separated in January 1973. She remained, with the children, at 46 Lower Belgrave Street; he moved out, but not far away, eventually to a basement flat, 72a, in Elizabeth Street, which runs from the western side of Eaton Square to the coach terminus in Buckingham Palace Road.

The schism, in itself expensive for Lucan, was made more so by two of his subsequent acts. In March 1973 – perhaps on the spur of the moment, having seen his children being exercised by the current nanny while he was walking through Green Park, heading for or coming from a club – he inveigled two of the children from their minder, took them to his flat, and kept them there for several weeks, during which time lawyers representing him argued with lawyers representing his wife over which of them was best suited as custodian of all three children. Dirty linen was washed in public – not in a cheap, launderettish way, but at a cost of £40,000. The arbitrating judge made the children wards of court, but said that, so long as Veronica employed a mindful nanny (paid for by Lucan), custody should remain with her. Lucan was furious at the decision; distressed (and, for once, one can feel sympathy towards him) by the lawyers' bills.

Instead of making the best of what to him was a bad job, he hired a private investigator to spy on Veronica. Presumably his hope was that the man would witness her doing something, or a number of things, so outrageously unmaternal that the custody case could be re-opened, the first decision reversed. A forlorn hope, surely, if only because she so rarely left the house: she would have had to be more unbalanced than he had persuaded himself she was, and exhibitionistically so, to behave grotesquely in full view of someone looking at the windows of 46 Lower Belgrave Street from a diagonal distance. And – unless she was unobservant of regular loiterers near the house, or unless the private investigator was subtler or more versatile of disguise than the majority of his sleazy kind – the surveillance could easily have been counter-productive, warning her to refrain from outlandishness except when the satin curtains were tight-closed. Neither the duration of the investigator's investigation nor the contents of his reports to Lucan seems to be known; but going by what Lucan divulged to an habitué of the Clermont, the investigator's weekly hire-charge, which had to be paid in cash on demand, was sometimes in the region of £400.

Either off Lucan's own bat or at the investigator's suggestion, he acquired a slim-line tape-recorder, stowed it in a waistcoat pocket before visiting the house, and there sought to infuriate Veronica into fits of hysterics. Afterwards, he would play edited versions of the recordings – his vexing contributions excised – to gambling cronies, commenting in a what-did-I-tell-you way the while. As months passed, his commentaries were more and more larded with long words – defined by himself to his own satisfaction but mysterious to most of his audience – that he had culled from DIY-psychiatry books; he applied most of the words to Veronica's 'condition', the rest to the unpeacefulness of his own mind that he accused her of causing. He had a helper in trying to distress his wife – a person who made anonymous telephone calls to her, some of them threatening, others of a sexually perverted nature. Why he didn't make the calls himself, or get his helper to make them on the listed number rather than on an ex-directory number that was known only to himself and Veronica (because the line was linked to an alarm-gadget on the safe in the house), will never be surely explained. So far as is known, he did not record the telephone calls (supposing that he was not an *écouteur* of sadism, it would have been a waste of tape for him to have done so, since the recordings would have had evidential value to him only if Veronica's share of the conversations had *not* been hysterical), but he did record conversations with chatterbox nannies whom he enticed to his flat in Elizabeth Street, and with his children when he took them on joy-rides in the new Mercedes that – with a prodigality that, considering his financial situation, smacks more of insanity than of recklessness – he had borrowed money, at a high interest-rate, to buy.

After the settling of the legal bills, his accounts with several English banks were either reduced to nil-balances or overdrawn. If he did not win a lot more at gambling than he lost at it, he would soon be unable to meet regular commitments, which included school-fees for his two eldest children, the rent and upkeep of his flat (£2500 a year), the expenses of the house, an agreed annual allowance of £2000 to his wife, £1300 a year for nannies (that sum set by the Chancery judge), repayments on behalf of the Mercedes (cash-price, about £4500).

A gambling variant on Murphy's Law has it that the most likely loser is the player who most needs to win. Lucan seems to have exemplified the adage. Or perhaps there is something in what a one-time casino-owner, now a zoo-keeper, has said: 'There is nothing worse for a gambler than an unstable situation on his home ground. That wrecked Lucan's capacity to survive as a gambler. He lost a bit of his nerve and ability.'

He was now chain-smoking; drinking vodka as if it were Perrier water, sometimes using the vodka to swill down small pink pills that may or may not have been prescribed by his doctor as a means of diminishing the suffusion of his features. The Clermont was no longer pretending to be what, in the 1960s, it had masqueraded as: a gentlemen's club where games were played. It had been taken over by the American owner of a bottomless (as opposed to topless) club, members of which were allowed to use the Clermont – detrimentally to the place, in the view of most of the fully-fledged Clermontians, one of whom complained of the 'hideous' newcomers: 'They just take up space and are unpleasant for people to sit with.' And whereas in the good old days anyone not wearing a tie would have been refused admittance, there were now no vestmental grounds for exclusion: indeed, arabically-attired arabs – 'ludicrously got up for London, what with their nightgowns, mob-caps and sandals' – were more cosseted by the management than were suit-wearing 'Mid-Eastern punters', less likely to be 'oilionaires'. The new regime was displeasing to Lucan: not simply because of the influx of 'plebs', or 'wogs'; not merely because of the abolition of the 'free list', composed of the names of members who played so frequently, staked so high, that they were given lunch on the house – but, saliently, because the management didn't look upon him as 'good furniture', didn't give a hoot for his title, which, so far as they were financially concerned, was a lot less impressive than *Sheikh*, small change compared with *Emir*. He was given signs that he was no longer regarded as 'good furniture' when, a cheque for £10,000 that he had made out to the club having bounced, he was told that he had to remedy the error within twenty-four hours (which he just managed to do, following a whip-round among IOU-collecting friends) and that, until he provided proof of pecuniary resources, he would not be allowed credit.

The indignity was hard to take. He blamed it upon Veronica. Just as he blamed all of the other indignities upon her. And all of his misfortunes – every single one. His money troubles. His run of rotten luck at the tables. The loss of his children.

He invented a superstition: his misfortunes would continue,

would grow worse, would multiply, taking him to the depths and degrading the name of Lucan, unless the evil influence on his life were eradicated.

He didn't see – or refused to admit that he saw – that the superstition was lunatic: similar to a belief that, by making firewood of a ladder, thus eliminating the risk of walking under it, he would all of a sudden be carefree.

He had no choice, he decided. Veronica had to be murdered.

There was no doubt in his mind that he could do it; none that he could get away with it. After all, he had read enough thrillers to know everything there was to know about alibis, the making of weapons that didn't look like weapons, casual behaviour before the crime, shocked demeanour when told of it . . . things like that. Precise planning – that was what was needed. Same style as that of his military forebears. He had almost unique advantages by comparison with killers from among the hoi polloi – extra aces, so to say. His congenital brilliance as a tactician would make the execution a doddle, but in the unlikely event that not all went quite as expected, his iron determination to protect the Lucan name would make him irresistible to obstacles.

By the third weekend of October 1974, the plan was complete. He spoke of his intent to a friend. Since the friend was nearly as aristocratic as he was, he didn't embarrass him by putting him on his honour to respect a confidence. He explained that he was not merely skint: he was up to his eyes in debt and had run out of 'loan-sources'. In a month or so, Christie's would auction some of the family silver – but even if the sale went well, the proceeds would be like an aspirin to cure a cancer. He didn't want his son George to see him in a bankruptcy court – that would be appalling. So, no two ways about it, he had to get rid of Veronica. The friend pointed out apparent flaws in the reasoning. Surely George would be upset at being made motherless by his father . . .? And wouldn't he, if given the choice, prefer his father to be a declared bankrupt rather than a convicted murderer . . .? Lucan ignored the first objection, and rebutted the second by saying that he would not be caught.

Next day, or the day after, he began preparations. He approached another friend, Michael Stoop, who was a dab-hand at backgammon, asking if he might borrow his Ford Corsair. He didn't offer a reason; didn't explain what was wrong with his Mercedes. Stoop, a friend indeed, afterwards recalled: 'I suggested he should borrow my Mercedes as my Ford was dirty and an old banger, but he said he would take the Ford. I imagined it was just his natural manners that he asked for the Ford because he didn't want to deprive me of my better car.' Stoop arranged to leave the Ford outside his garage, with the keys in the glove-compartment, and Lucan drove it away. The car was untidy with odds and ends – none of which, so far as its owner was aware, was a length of lead piping.

On Thursday, 7 November, Lucan still had the car. Although he had been at the Clermont till the small hours, drinking even more heavily than usual while he gambled, he rose earlier than was his wont. At 9.50, he telephoned his solicitor; only the latter knows why. At 10.30, a young woman of his recent acquaintance telephoned him, asking about his dinner plans, and, finding them 'rather a muddle', rang off, thinking that when she saw him at the Clermont at lunch-time, she would ask again. But he didn't turn up at the club for his previously-invariable smoked salmon and lamb cutlets. No one seems to know what he was doing, or where he was, until four in the afternoon, when he went into a chemist's shop, seeking to identify a pill that he said he had taken from his wife, and, having been told that it was a tranquilliser, left – without having purchased anything, not even a roll of Elastoplast, the chemist subsequently told the police. He returned to the flat in Elizabeth Street, there to receive hints on journalism from Michael Hicks Beach, a friend from schooldays who had fixed up for him to write an article on gambling for an Oxford magazine. He drank while Hicks advised; then, using the Corsair, drove Hicks to his home in Fulham, had a few drinks with him, and drove back to the flat. Since, at night, it takes only five minutes or so to drive from Elizabeth Street to Berkeley Square, one is safe in saying that he had exchanged his suit, shirt and tie for grey flannel trousers, a roll-neck silk shirt and a brown pullover by about half-past eight, when he telephoned the Clermont to book a dinner-table for four at half-past ten. Within fifteen minutes of making the call, he was outside the Clermont, having driven to Berkeley Square in his Mercedes, and was enquiring of Billy, the doorman, whether his four dinner-guests had arrived.

To his way of thinking, the telephone call to the club and the enquiry of the doorman furnished him with an alibi for the murder that he was now going to commit at 46 Lower Belgrave Street. If Lucan had ever been tried for his crime, defence counsel would surely have used the 'alibi', not in an attempt to show that he was absent from the house when the murder took place, but as the main ground for a submission that he was an idiot, dead right for the secure home for the mentally deranged at Broadmoor as opposed to any of Her Majesty's prisons. Having at about 8.30 booked a table for 10.30, at about 8.45 he was asking whether his four guests had appeared – although, as could have been proved, he knew perfectly well that the guests were at the Mermaid Theatre, Blackfriars, enjoying the performance, not yet interrupted by an interval, of a compilation of songs by Cole Porter. Incidentally, the earlier reference to a table for *four* is correct: probably because Lucan's mind was so tired from the effort of thinking up an excuse for telephoning the Clermont and then calling there, it had completely escaped him that four guests plus the host makes five. When the guests arrived, at 10.45, and were ushered to a table sufficient only for themselves, they asked for a fifth place to be laid; an hour later, still mystifyingly hostless, they ordered. By then, Lucan, unwittingly following the advice of a song his paying guests had heard earlier in the evening, had got out of town – forty miles out, as far as Uckfield.

His presence in that Sussex town was the result of a hash of blunders, the first and most hideous of which was due to his inclusion of a false assumption in his murder-plan.

He chose a Thursday night for the crime because he *knew* that his children's nanny *always* had Thursday night off. That meant, of course, that the coast would be clear: by about nine, the children would be asleep in their rooms at the top of the house; there would be no interference, no witness, when he battered his wife to death.

It seems unlikely that he had ever seen the present nanny, for she had been in the job only a few weeks. Her name was Sandra Eleanor Rivett, *née* Hensby. She was twenty-nine, a native of Basingstoke, separated from her husband, who was a security guard at Gatwick Airport; her small son was looked after by her parents. She was a pretty woman, the same height but plumper than her new mistress; her hair was naturally auburn, crisper than Veronica's but worn in a similar, centrally-parted, style. She had had several jobs, none lasting long, since the break-up of her marriage; most recently, she had been the living-in servant of an elderly couple in Paddington. In the short time she had been at 46 Lower Belgrave Street, she had got to know and become friendly with a locum manager of the nearby Plumbers' Arms. He had asked her out on the night of Wednesday, 6 November. Veronica hadn't minded her taking her weekly evening-off a day early.

The importance of television as an aid to criminal investigation, fixing times of incidents with some degree of accuracy, is illustrated by the statement of the Lucan's eldest child, ten-year-old Frances, regarding the events of the Thursday night:

> At 7.20 I watched *Top of the Pops* in the nursery. Mummy, Camilla, George and Sandra were downstairs [on the second floor] watching *The Six Million Dollar Man*. I joined them at 8.05 [*Top of the Pops* having ended just before eight] and we all watched TV in Mummy's room. When the programme finished at 8.30 I went back to the nursery and played with my games. Sandra brought Camilla and George upstairs and put them to bed. I had had my bath and was wearing my pyjamas. I stayed in the nursery about five minutes. I went downstairs again to Mummy's room about 8.40. I asked Mummy where Sandra was and Mummy said she was downstairs [in the basement-kitchen] making tea. After a while Mummy said she wondered why Sandra was so long. It was before the news came on at 9 p.m. I said I would go downstairs to see what was keeping her, but Mummy said no, she would go down. She left the bedroom door open, but there was no light in the hall. Just after Mummy left the room I heard a scream. It sounded as though it came from a long way away. I thought perhaps the cat had scratched Mummy and she had screamed. I was not frightened. I went to the door and called Mummy but there was no answer and I left it. At 9.05 the news was on TV and Daddy and Mummy both walked into the room. Mummy had blood over her face and was crying. Mummy told me to go upstairs. Daddy didn't say anything to me and I said nothing to either of them. I don't know how much blood was on her face. I didn't hear any conversation between Mummy and Daddy. I didn't see any blood on Daddy's clothes. I wondered what had happened but I didn't ask.

According to Veronica,[1] what had happened was this:

She had gone down to the hall, which was in darkness ('. . . we had not replaced the light-bulbs as they burned out; this was an economy of mine to fend off any suggestions of extravagance from

---

[1] Most of the quotations in the following three paragraphs are from the *Daily Express* of 20 January 1975.

my estranged husband'), and walked to the top of the stairs leading to the basement. Looking down, she saw that the kitchen-light
was not on. 'I was puzzled because I knew that Sandra couldn't be
making tea in the dark.' (Subsequently, it was found that the bulb
had been taken out. A bulb was lying on a chair.) She called out the
nanny's name. Twice. 'Then behind me I heard a rustling noise. It
came from the ground-floor cloakroom. . . . I turned towards the
sound. Suddenly there was something rushing at me out of the
cloakroom . . . I was struck at least four times on the right side of
my forehead. I couldn't see who it was but he was much taller than
me. . . . I screamed as loudly as I possibly could. It wasn't just the
pain but the whole terror of the attack in the pitch-darkness. The
man thrust three gloved fingers down my throat and said, "Shut
up." I recognised the voice as that of my husband. As I fought
back, he attempted to strangle me and then to gouge out my left eye
with his thumb. . . . We fell into the basement stairway, and in the
struggle I managed to hook my leg through the bars of the banister-
rail. I was getting to the stage by then that I felt I couldn't struggle
any more. I can remember thinking to myself, "I'm going. I'm
going." And my next thought was, "I'm going to die at thirty-
seven. A bit young to die." She grabbed Lucan by the genitals and
squeezed with all her might. That caused him to let go of her. He
sat on a step, panting, whimpering, cradling his private parts. 'I
asked him, "Where is the nanny?" The answer came: "She's gone
out." I insisted: "But she wouldn't have gone out without telling
me." Then he muttered: "She is dead." I now knew that I had to
play for time and think up some plan for escaping. So I replied:
"Oh, dear, what shall we do with the body?" He mumbled: "She is
downstairs – but don't look. She is a horrid sight – an awful mess."
. . . I asked if I could have a glass of water. He let me go into the
cloakroom, where I got a drink. He asked me at that point if I had
any sleeping pills. When I replied that I had some, he asked me if I
would take them. I suppose to finish the job. I said I would. Then
he took me up to my bedroom.'

Once Frances had gone, he turned off the television. Veronica
said that she wanted to lie down on the bed. He went into the
bathroom.

'When the taps started running, I knew that he would be temporarily deafened. So I jumped to my feet and ran down the stairs.
My heart was pumping to bursting point. I felt sick and exhausted,

but I threw myself out of the front door and into the street. There was not a soul around. I ran to the public house which I often went to during an evening for cigarettes.'

Perhaps because of the drizzling rain, the staff of The Plumbers' Arms were not much outnumbered by customers. As there was no television set in the bar, no one was afterwards able, reconstructively, to put a time to when the door burst open and a slight, barefoot woman, blood disfiguring her face, staggered towards the counter. 'Help me, help me,' she screamed. 'I've just escaped from a murderer. My children . . . my children. . . . He's in the house. He has murdered the nanny.'

Next day, the landlord would tell a reporter, 'That kind of thing doesn't usually happen around here' – a comment that, while not intended as an excuse for any tardiness in dialling 999 and asking for an ambulance and the police, in that order, may explain why the first message to police cars cruising in the area did not go out till one minute past ten.

By the time that two uniformed officers forced open the door of 46 Lower Belgrave Street, Veronica (who, after her outburst upon entering the pub, had said who she was, but nothing else that was comprehensible) had been taken in an ambulance to St. George's Hospital at Hyde Park Corner (where she would remain, receiving treatment of her injuries and for shock, for six days).

Lucan had gone from the house. The only living people there were his children: all were in rooms on the top floor, George and Camilla sound asleep, Frances standing, frightened and bewildered, near her sister's bed. She told a policeman something of what had happened. The police transferred light-bulbs from rooms that could afford the loss to the hall and basement, and began a search.

The corpse of Sandra Rivett was doubled up inside a United States mail-bag that lay on the floor of the breakfast room in the basement. (Had Lucan brought the canvas bag with him – perhaps intending it as a coffin for the woman he meant to murder and then carry from the house – or was it already there? I cannot tell.) Subsequently, a pathologist, Professor Keith Simpson, examined the body and found six splits in the head, four of them in the region of the front hair-line; severe bruising, caused by blows, on both shoulders; slighter bruising, which may have been either defence-wounds or the result of strong finger-pressure, on the right arm.

On the half-landing of the basement stairway was a piece of lead piping, 9 inches long and weighing 2¼ pounds, neatly wrapped round with Elastoplast. It was heavily bloodstained. There was no doubt that it had been used to kill Sandra Rivett, to inflict the wounds on Lady Lucan's head. None of the investigators, some of whom had seen some very strange murder-weapons, could explain the Elastoplast wrapping.

There were splashes of blood on the steps between the hall and the half-landing, on the proximate wall and banisters (two adjacent bars of which were distorted), and on the low ceiling directly above. There was much blood in the basement – most noticeable, a puddle at the foot of the stairs, near the door to the kitchen; in and around it were broken cups and saucers, presumably dropped by the nanny when she was attacked.

In the main bedroom, a wet towel, slightly stained with blood, was draped across the pillows on the double bed.

By twenty minutes past ten, when the first detectives arrived at the house, the uniformed constable who had spoken to Frances had compared notes with a colleague who had observed the bloodstained towel. They had concluded that the material evidence supported the child's scrappy account of what had happened after the nanny had gone to the kitchen to make tea. (I have quoted only the first part of Frances's statement. She went on to say that, some time after she had been sent to her room, she heard her father call out, 'Veronica, where are you?' Looking over the banisters, she saw him come out of the main bedroom, run to the bathroom on the same floor, then go downstairs. 'That was the last I saw of him. He never came up to the top of the house either to look for Mummy or to say good-night to me.')

The senior detective, a sergeant, conferred with the uniformed constables, and then looked for a clue to Lord Lucan's whereabouts. Having come across a document showing that 5 Eaton Row, a mews-cottage round the corner from Lower Belgrave Street, belonged to a Lucan family trust, he went there, but found no one at home. It was eleven o'clock when he returned to the house. Meanwhile, the Dowager Countess of Lucan had arrived. She explained that she had received a telephone call from her son: 'He said that there had been a terrible catastrophe at No. 46. He said, "Veronica is hurt, and I want you to collect the children as quickly as possible." He also said – and he might have said this first – "Ring

Bill Shand-Kydd, and he will help." He also said the nanny was hurt, and I asked, "Badly?" He said, "Yes, I think so."' The Dowager Countess added that her son had told her that 'he was driving past the house and he saw a fight going on in the basement between a man and Veronica. He went in and joined them. He said Veronica was shouting and screaming.' (Tests subsequently carried out by the police showed that only tiny slices of the kitchen could be seen by anyone driving past the house and looking at the part of the basement window – covered by a Venetian blind – that was visible above the pavement. And, of course, if there was no light in the kitchen, virtually none of the room could be seen: in order not to disbelieve Lucan's tale, it was necessary to believe that the kitchen was lit when he looked through the window but that, by the time he joined in the fight, either Veronica or her foe had broken off combat, unscrewed the bulb, placed the bulb on a chair, then started fighting again.)

The Dowager Countess took her grandchildren to her flat overlooking Lord's cricket ground in St. John's Wood. A police constable went with them. He was still in the flat after midnight, when the telephone rang. He heard the Dowager Countess say to the caller: 'Where are you? . . . Are you all right? . . . Yes, they are all safe here and are asleep. . . . Well, look, the police are here – do you want to speak to them?' Replacing the receiver, she told the constable: 'That was my son. He won't speak to you now. He will phone you in the morning.'

He did not keep that promise.

Detective Chief Superintendent Roy Ranson, who from first thing on Friday headed what came to be called the 'Nob Squad' of detectives investigating the crime, waited all day for Lord Lucan to telephone.

Lucan's silence – permanent, as it turned out – is more understandable than the temporary silence of acquaintances who had seen or heard from him after his visit to the family home.

One of the acquaintances was a woman called Madeleine Florman, who lived in Chester Square, just west of Lower Belgrave Street; her daughter attended the same school as Lucan's daughter Frances. Within an hour of the murder, her doorbell was rung persistently – but, so she eventually told the police, she was too frightened to answer it. A few minutes later, she received a telephone call from a man – Lucan, she was sure – who said, 'Madeleine, I know you. . . .', but then hung up. Mrs. Florman waited six days before reporting the incidents to the police, mentioning in passing that there were some nasty brown stains on her nice white doorstep. The stains were tested and found to be of blood.

Another of the acquaintances was a woman called Susan Maxwell Scott, who lived on the outskirts of Uckfield (coincidentally close to where Veronica had spent her early years), at a fine house that her husband had bought after a spectacular gambling coup; the husband had known, and played with, Lucan for twenty years. Mrs. Scott, who was the daughter of a Queen's Counsel, had qualified as a solicitor but had never practised. She was alone on the Thursday night; had gone to bed at eleven, and was not yet asleep when the doorbell rang. Having looked out of the window and seen Lucan standing by the porch, she let him in. He was 'a little dishevelled'; there was a 'wet patch' on the right hip of his grey flannel trousers. After giving him a Scotch and water, 'I asked him what was the matter. He told me what had happened at his wife's house. He said he had been walking past the house on his way to change for dinner. . . . I am almost certain he used the word "walking". He told me that on looking through the Venetian blind in the basement he saw a man attacking his wife, so he let himself in with his door-key and went down to the basement. As he entered the corridor, he slipped in a pool of blood. He was not telling this like a story. It came out in bits, and this is my best attempt to tell you what he said to me. The man he had seen attacking his wife ran off. . . . Lucan, perhaps unfortunately, refrained from chasing the man but went to his wife. . . . He said first she was very hysterical and cried out to him that someone had killed the nanny, then almost in the same breath accused Lucan of having hired the man to kill *her*. . . . He took her upstairs. It was his intention to get some towels to mop up the blood and see how bad it was, then to telephone the doctor and then the police. He said he felt rather squeamish with the blood. He went to the bathroom and started soaking the towels, but while he was there Lady Lucan left the bedroom, ran down the stairs and out of the house. . . . He said he felt that there he was, alone in the house, the dead body, all that blood, and a wife gone away who would almost certainly try to implicate him.'

Having told Mrs. Scott all that, he telephoned his mother (presumably this was the call made while the constable was at the Dowager Countess's home), and then wrote two letters to William Shand-Kydd, sealed them in separate envelopes, and asked Mrs. Scott to post them. He turned down her invitation to stay, saying that he had to 'get back' to clear things up. It was a quarter past one when he drove off in a dark saloon-car.

The two letters were delivered to William Shand-Kydd, at his home in Bayswater, on Saturday morning. The notepaper of both of them was stained, perhaps with blood. Some time after their arrival, Mr. Shand-Kydd told the police about them. One read as follows:

Dear Bill,
The most ghastly circumstances arose tonight, which I have described briefly to my mother, when I interrupted the fight at Lower Belgrave Street and the man left.
V. accused me of having hired him. I took her upstairs and sent Frances to bed and tried to clean her up. She lay doggo for a bit. I went into the bathroom and she left the house.
The circumstantial evidence against me is strong in that V. will say it was all my doing and I will lie doggo for a while, but I am only concerned about the children. If you can manage it I would like them to live with you.
V. has demonstrated her hatred for me in the past and would do anything to see me accused.
For George and Frances to go through life knowing their father had been in the dock accused of attempted murder would be too much for them.
When they are old enough to understand explain to them the dream of paranoia and look after them.

LUCKY

(Months later, a lawyer asked Mr. Shand-Kydd if he could explain the term 'dream of paranoia'. He said that he could, but was told not to.)

The other letter, which was headed 'FINANCIAL MATTERS', began:

There is going to be a sale at Christie's which will rectify the bank overdraft. Please agree reserves herein.

Then came a list of items of family silver, with Lucan's estimate of the value of each. The letter ended:

Proceeds to go to Lloyds, Coutts, and National Westminster – and the other creditors can get lost for the time being.

JOHN

(Lucan's overdraft at Lloyds, Pall Mall, was £4379; at Coutts, in the Strand, it was £2841; at the National Westminster, Bloomsbury Way, it was £1291. Among the creditors who, Lucan felt, could get lost for the time being was a fourth bank, the Midland, in Newgate Street, where he had an overdraft of £5667, and a firm of moneylenders at Bexleyheath, Kent, from whom he had recently borrowed £3000 at interest of £120 a month, equivalent to 48 per cent per annum, having persuaded a friend to guarantee the loan.)

Chief Superintendent Ranson was less intrigued by the contents of the letters than by the 'UCKFIELD' postmark on the envelopes. He had discovered that **THE MISSING EARL** (as Lucan was being headlined) had borrowed Michael Stoop's Ford Corsair; but, till now (if press accounts are accurate), he had concentrated the Earlhunt within London, doing little more in a provincial way than to alert police and Customs officers at airports and ferry-embarkation harbours. Perhaps he had misled by the anonymous telephoners, reporting sightings of Lucan in one Mayfair club or another; some of the callers may have believed that they were being helpful, some were practised hoaxers for pleasure, but most, it seems, were acquaintances of Lucan, members of the 'Eton Mafia', indulging in what Ranson afterwards described as 'the horseplay of the upper classes'. Ranson detailed one of the Nob Squad to find out whether Lucan had Uckfield connections, and thus learned of the Scotts. Detectives despatched to the Scotts' house took a statement from the house's mistress. Asked why she had not gone to the police, she replied languidly: 'I had no reason to.' And, what with her legal parentage and training, no one argued with her.

According to Mrs. Scott, she had invited Lucan to stay the night but he had said that he had to 'get back' to clear things up. If he *had* returned to London in the early hours of Friday, any effort he had made to clear things up during the following day and a half had been entirely unobtrusive, so far as the Metropolitan Police were concerned. And his excuse to Mrs. Scott was hard to reconcile with the words, 'I will lie doggo for a while,' in one of his letters to Mr. Shand-Kydd; almost impossible to reconcile with his thoughts about his children's long-term future in the last sentence of the same letter.

Ranson sent out an all-forces request that officers should keep a look-out for Lord Lucan and a dark-blue Ford Corsair, registration number KJN 135D.

At three o'clock on Sunday afternoon, Ranson heard that the car had been found parked in a quiet residential street in Newhaven, on the Sussex coast, twelve miles south of Uckfield. From subsequent inquiries of early-rising local people, the Newhaven police gathered that the car had not been there before five o'clock on Friday morning.

There were smears of blood on both of the front seats, on the steering wheel and dashboard, and on the inside of the driver's door. Also inside the car was a full bottle of vodka. The locked boot contained a piece of lead piping, two feet long, wrapped round with Elastoplast: the piping looked identical to that used as the murder weapon; an end of each piece had been cut with a hacksaw, leaving traces of blue paint.

Samples of blood from the car were sent to the Metropolitan Police Forensic Science Laboratory, where Dr. Margaret Pereira, the principal scientific officer, had already begun classifying blood from the house and from the victims. Basically, her findings were as follows. Blood from the basement was of group B (as was Sandra Rivett's – among, it was reckoned, 8.5 per cent of the population); that from the end of the hall and top of the basement steps was of group A (as was Lady Lucan's – among, it was reckoned, 42 per cent of the population). Some of the blood from the Elastoplast on the weapon was of group A, some was of group B, and some gave a reaction to AB – indicating that it was either of that group or a mixture of A and B. The same was true of blood from the car.

Dr. Pereira's blood-groupings were of less evidential value than her conclusion that greyish-blue wool fibres found in the car were 'microscropically indistinguishable' from fibres found about the house and on the weapon.

A fingerprint on the rear-view mirror in the car was almost certainly Lucan's. It matched fingerprints in his flat that differed from those of Michael Stoop and some other persons who had visited him.

On Monday afternoon, Mr. Stoop telephoned the police from the St. James's Club, saying that, upon his arrival there, he had been handed a letter from Lucan. He agreed to drop the letter in at the Gerald Street police station, the Nob Squad's headquarters – and did so at three o'clock next morning. The letter, written on paper similar to some found in the glove-compartment of the Ford Corsair, read as follows:

My dear Michael,

I have had a traumatic night of unbelievable coincidence. However, I won't bore you with anything to involve you except to say that when you come across my children, which I hope you will, please tell them that you knew me and that all I cared about was them. I gave Bill Shand-Kydd an account of what actually happened, but judging by my last effort in court no one, let alone a 67-year-old judge, would believe – and I no longer care, except that my children should be protected.

Yours ever,

JOHN

When Mr. Stoop was asked for the envelope, he said that he had thrown it away at the club. He said that he had not noticed the postmark. All that he remembered, he said, was that the envelope was large and white – and that, as it had been unstamped (perhaps delaying delivery), the doorman had paid the postage due.

Policeman were sent to the club to search through refuse containers. In view of the fact that there had been no refuse collection for some days, it is strange to say that the envelope did not come to light.

The letter to Michael Stoop was the last that was heard from Lord Lucan.

A few hours after the letter was read by Chief Superintendent Ranson, a magistrate signed two warrants for the arrest of Lucan, one alleging that he had killed Sandra Rivett, the other alleging that he had tried to kill his wife. In the following June, an inquest jury listened to evidence that a coroner, Dr. Gavin Thurston, had filleted of controversial bits, took merely half an hour to discuss it, and then returned the verdict that Lucan had murdered his children's nanny. Several relatives and friends of the murderer were quoted as saying that he was as innocent of murder as they were, but none was arrested on suspicion. In 1977, the jury's verdict was made historic, as the last individual-accusing one in a coroner's court, by a section of a Criminal Law Act.

Meanwhile, Lord Lucan look-alikes had had a hard time; and so had some men who looked nothing like him. Sightings of him had been reported from, among other places, Bogota, Bridgetown, Cairo, Capetown, Cherbourg, Las Vegas, and Maputo (which, I should explain, is in Mozambique). If he had been alive, he would not have been well pleased about some of the misidentifications of him: two in Melbourne, for instance, the first of a recently-arrived Englishman who turned out to be a former Labour government minister named John Stonehouse, pretending to be someone else after faking his death from drowning off the coast of Florida so as to avoid punishment for financial shenanigans, and the second of another recently-arrived Englishman, whose name of Kenneth *Knight* gave rise to suspicion, and whose assertion that he was not a professional gambler but a master boilermaker was pooh-poohed by the arresting officers, feelers of his baby-soft hands, until his wife, whom he had left behind in a pebble-dashed, bijou residence in Essex, when shown a snap of him, had tittered, 'That's not the Lord of Lucan – that's my Ken, that is.'

If one discards the conjecture that some of Lucan's wealthy acquaintances clubbed together to keep him in a secure but cosy place, minded night and day by warders, the notion that he survived for long following his drive to Newhaven – that, even now, he is arrestable – is as nonsensical as the notion that John Dillinger evaded an FBI ambush in 1934, and was able to live, out of sight if not out of mind, till a natural ailment accounted for him. The psychopathic, publicity-adoring Dillinger, as proud of his unofficial crowning as King Gaol-Breaker as of his official title of Public Enemy Number One, would have been incapable of staying secluded: if he had been around to read his obituary notices, he could not have resisted drawing attention to their prematurity – proving by words or misdeeds that he was a living legend. The reckless, gambling-obsessed Lucan, who would have done better as a murderer, might even have got the victim right, if he had not premeditated the crime, would have been incapable of staying away from the tables. Prevented from using his title as a shield against nonentity, unable to make money in a legitimate way, he would have been forced to gamble. Writers about Dillinger and writers about Lucan have contended that their respective subjects could have tinkered with, added to, or subtracted from their features so that no one would recognise them – but, so far as Lucan is concerned, the idea is flatly contradicted by a collection of doctored photographs of him that Roy Ranson, now retired from the police, keeps on the wall of his present place of employment: whether Mandarin-moustached, bearded, clean-shaven, bespectacled, grey-haired, coiffured like a rock star, or what, Lucan looks exactly like Lucan.

Perhaps he went out in a boat from Newhaven for the purpose of jumping overboard. The sea off the Sussex coast is said to be a favourite spot for and means of suicide – troublesomely to fishermen, some of whom, rather than report a netted body, which means confiscation of their catch and impoundment of their boat, pierce the swollen stomach and despatch the body to the deep. An authority on the eating habits of Crustacea reckons that a good-sized body, dropped conveniently to seawater crabs – of which there are thousands off Newhaven – will be fleshless within two or three days. My stomach is not turned by the thought that transmuted remnants of the Clermont's most celebrated member may have gone back to the club, there to be devilled as a speciality of the restaurant, and munched obliviously by diners, maybe reminiscing about him between mouthfuls.

It is a shame, though only in a minor respect, that the location of whatever may be left of him remains unknown. The suggestion for an epitaph for an earlier card-playing and absconding nobleman, Lord De Ros, could be varied thus:

> HERE LIES LORD LUCAN –
> in confident expectation
> of the Last Trump.

Postscript

In October 1985, Nicholas Boyce, a 38-year-old philosophy graduate of the London School of Economics, who had last been employed as a charperson at a doss-house near where Dr. Crippen fragmented Belle Elmore, stood trial at the Old Bailey for the murder of his wife Christabel, who was six years younger than himself.

The jury heard undisputed evidence that Boyce, irritated (*inter alia*) by Christabel's wish that he should give up smoking, had beaten her, butted her, and strangled her with a length of heavy-duty fuse-wire; that, after making sure that the two small children of the marriage were sound asleep, he, an adamant vegetarian, had hacked the corpse into approximately one hundred portions, boiled some of them so as to look like 'the remains of Sunday lunch' and popped the rest into polythene bags (a certain fastidiousness had prohibited him from winkling the contact lenses from the extremely bloodshot eyes); that, taking the children with him on most occasions, he had dribbled the dismemberments about London – off bridges, into marshes, into bins at the rear of a McDonald's junk-food establishment; that, having told the police one story, all to do with self-defence, he had felt impelled – because of discoveries made by forensic scientists – to utter a revised version, and then, when that was shown to be false in a salient respect, to try again.

Rules governing hearsay evidence forbade the Crown from attempting to rebut Boyce's plea of provocation on the unsubstantiated ground that Christabel had subjected him to 'mental torture', and the jury, which was composed equally of men and women, found him guilty only of manslaughter. Thereupon, the judge, Sir James Miskin, Recorder of London, sentenced him to six years in prison. According to a report in *The Daily Telegraph*, 'Boyce allowed himself a smile' at that. So long as he does nothing atrociously illegal in the meantime, he should be released on parole before Lent, 1987.

One paper – not, of course, the *Telegraph* – invented 'The Lucan Curse' when it became known that, in the early 1970s, Christabel, then a sort of locum-nanny of Belgravia, had once or twice stood in as nanny to the Lucan children. Her diary for 1974 having been found among her possessions, it was described by reporters as her *secret* diary – for no other reason than because she had never thought of giving public readings from it. Several papers squandered yards of column-space on the quotation of entries regarding the Lucan case, these beneath headlines of the now-it-can-be-told sort. In fact, the entries were singularly unrevelatory, mostly culled from the papers of the time or noting snatches of Belgravian gossip, founded on guesswork. Interviewed for a television programme, Lady Lucan – whose face seemed to have received the attention of a colour-blind make-up girl, for her eyes, brows as well, were daubed with blue mascara, and a similarly blue beauty-spot blemished one of her cheeks – had to rack her brains to recall, but then only vaguely, who Christabel was.

The Deadly Inheritance

Since much of the thrivingness of most insurance companies is derived, first, from their policy-printers' skill at giving myriad provisos less than their typographic due, and second, when claims arise, from their assessors' siftings through the printers' tidy dust of one-point grey italic for excuses for subtractions from the promised sums, it is not surprising that people who shy from sanctimony, when claiming, are tempted to overstate their losses, and when hearing of endeavours to deceive the companies, *usually* require reasons aside from the deceptions for not wishing the deceivers well. I stressed the word 'usually' because most virtuous persons draw the line of disapproval at attempts to outwit the companies that (I am speaking of the attempts) are reliant upon crime. When the crime relied upon is murder, the disapproval is practically unanimous, irrespective of whether the killing was done by a claimant or by someone acting on behalf of a claimant – or, as seems to have been so in the case of Baron Dieter von Schauroth, by someone who carried out the executional odd job at the request of the victim.

The following description of the aforementioned baron appeared in a report on the front page of the South African newspaper, the *Cape Argus*, published in the afternoon of Saturday, 25 March 1961:

> He is a swarthy, gaunt-faced European. . . . He is well-built and has dark-brown hair, slightly wavy, and brown eyes. He has a tiny gold stopping in a tooth next to the left eye-tooth and has a faint 1½-inch scar on the point of the chin. He was wearing green corduroy trousers, a brown corduroy jacket, a yellow and white checked open-necked shirt, bright-coloured socks and reddish-brown shoes. He could have been a farmer.

The Von Schauroths are a German family whose nobility stretches back to the start of the fourteenth century. By the end of the eighteenth century, the family owned twenty-seven estates in the area around Weimar; the sons became army officers or gentlemen-in-waiting in the dukedoms of Prussia, and the daughters married into other noble families. Subsequently, extravagance by some of the male Von Schauroths – not least, in aid of plain daughters or sisters whose hope of matrimony would have been forlorn had they lacked the attraction of large dowries – depleted the family fortunes to the extent that, by the 1850s, allowances to augment army salaries were so meagre that although all of the sons attended the military academy at Koblenz, few became soldiers or remained so for long. Many of the civilian Von Schauroths emigrated, some to neighbouring countries, others to the United States, Africa, and the Malay Archipelago.

The military tradition lingered on in one of the family lines. In 1896, Erich von Schauroth, the son of a general, was himself commissioned. On account of his aristocratic lineage, his height of six feet four inches, and his handsomeness, he was chosen to join the most elite regiment in the German army, the Elisabeth Grenadier Garde, stationed in Berlin. The posting did not please him, for the Garde's duties were chiefly ceremonial, and he was keen to see action. In 1900 he volunteered for service in China, protecting German concessions threatened by the Boxer Rebellion. After two years in China, he returned to Berlin. Just over a year later, he again volunteered for overseas service – this time in German South-West Africa, where native tribes, as well as warring against one another, were in revolt against the white administrators and colonists.

The revolt was not quelled till 1907 – by when, it is reckoned, the population of Hereros, told apart from the Hottentots by their relative tallness, had been reduced from 80,000 to 12,000, and some 1600 members of the expeditionary force had died from fever, stomach ailments, or battle-wounds. Lieutenant von Schauroth, unscathed, went back to Germany. His salient memory of the expedition was a peaceful one: of days spent with his troop in a valley, lush with grass, stippled with camelthorn trees, on the western hem of the Kalahari Desert, south of the Great Karas Mountains. Within the valley, a mile from where the land lurched up to make a small hill, was a well fed by water from a spring. Cape Dutchmen called the well Blinkoog because, when the sun's rays were at a particular angle, the damp stones seemed to blink like dazzled eyes.

Shortly after Von Schauroth's return from Africa, his father died. As well as succeeding to the title of Baron, he came into a small inheritance: money, a piece of land, most of the few remaining family treasures.

His memory of the green valley – all of it now called Blinkoog in his mind – was appended with a desire to own it, to build a castle in it, to make of it an estate more splendid than any that his family had ever owned. He wrote to the commissioner of the district that encompassed Blinkoog, asking if the valley could be purchased, and received the reply that the land formed the main part of a reserved holding of 50,000 acres that was available only to an ex-soldier who had been demobilised in the country; the price was about 15,000 marks (roughly £750), payable over eight years. Von Schauroth straightway applied for the holding, and as soon as he received word from the district commissioner that Blinkoog had been allotted to him, requested a posting to South-West Africa.

The request was eventually granted, and at the end of 1912, having settled his affairs in Germany and arranged shipment of heirlooms and of plundered souvenirs of his service in China, he set off on the long journey to the land that he had been promised. After arriving at Walvis Bay – the only good harbour between Angola, to the north, and the Orange River, which forms the boundary with South Africa – he travelled 170 miles east by train to the capital, Windhoek, and there whiled away the time till his application to be placed on the reserve of officers was accepted; then he made the two-day train-journey to the village of Karasburg, 450 miles to the south. During the next few days he bought horses, oxen, and a wagon, filled the wagon with provisions, cooking utensils, tools, and vegetable seed, and hired as his servant a thirty-year-old Hottentot called Yellow Boy who, though wizened of face and only five feet tall, was almost as strong as any of the oxen, and had the additional qualifications of familiarity with the area around Blinkoog and rudimentary skill at stone-cutting. The fifty-mile trek to Blinkoog, through the parched scrubland north-east of Karasburg, took four days. Although the valley must have been in some respects less perfect than the place Von Schauroth's memory had made increasingly sublime, he gazed upon it with entire delight.

Early on the first morning, he and Yellow Boy set to work. They did not labour alone for long. The arrival of the white man had been observed by local Hottentots, and two of them, made brave by hunger, approached and asked to be allowed to work in return for food. Almost as soon as Von Schauroth assented, eighteen more of the tiny people appeared, as if from nowhere, clamouring to be taken on. He had not intended to acquire livestock yet awhile, but felt obliged to, so as to honour his side of the working arrangement; and, leaving Yellow Boy in command, he rode back to Karasburg to buy bags of maize and beans – and more tools.

The money was well spent. Within a couple of months, the valley was patched with fields in which vegetable seed and maize had been sown. And trenches had been dug in a shelf in the central hillock; were being filled with the foundations of Von Schauroth's Castle. Already, Yellow Boy was cutting slabs of sandstone from a side of the valley, and these were being dragged by oxen to the base of the hillock, there to be pushed and pulled on to the shelf by the strongest of the Hottentots. After a further year or so, the walls of the lower floor of the Castle, each about forty feet long, were complete.

Meanwhile, Von Schauroth had visited, and had been visited by, his nearest neighbours, a Dutch family called Le Riche who were prospering from the breeding of caracul sheep, the black pelts of which were fetching a good price from fur-traders. He had become enamoured of the eldest daughter, Talita, and she of him.

By the early summer of 1914, the lower floor of the Castle had been divided into four rooms, covered by a temporary roof. In preparation for the move from the mud-hut that had been his mean abode for a year and a half, Von Schauroth increased the frequency of his trips to Karasburg from once a month (always on the day when he could draw what remained from his army pension after deduction of an instalment of the purchase-price of Blinkoog), bringing back with him the crates of his belongings shipped from Germany, and furniture, linen and household items that he had bought. Leaving most of the crates of heirlooms unpacked in one of the rooms, he furnished another and hung it about with pictures of great houses – none castles – that had once been in his family; also, symbolising his own past and present, his regimental sword of honour and a new rifle fit for killing deer. On a night in August, he slept in the Castle for the first time. Next day, he rode to Karasburg. There, he learned that Germany was at war with, among other European nations, Great Britain – and so with its dominions, which included the Union of South Africa.

He re-enlisted, of course. Returning to Blinkoog until his orders came through, he fashioned a flag-pole. Every morning he summoned the ragged Hottentots to stand in line while he raised a German flag and saluted it, and at the end of each day called them to an equally mystified sort of attention while he lowered it. More practically, he made a hiding-place for jewels left to him by his mother and a few gold coins that he had saved, and bricked up the door of the room containing the unopened crates. When he was told to report to the garrison at Windhoek, he dismissed the local Hottentots, gave Yellow Boy a note to obtain pay in Karasburg for looking after Blinkoog during his absence, and, having said good-bye to his Dutch neighbours, fondly to Talita, rode to Karasburg. Before taking the train going north to Windhoek, he gave the district commissioner two years' payment on his land.

The German troops were outnumbered by the invading South Africans, and in July 1915 their commander surrendered; subsequently, the country was administered under mandate by the Union.

Wearing civilian clothes and carrying a forged Swiss passport, Von Schauroth travelled across country towards the Portuguese colony of Mozambique, intending to board a neutral vessel bound for Germany. He was arrested and imprisoned, but managed to escape. Recaptured, he was taken to an internment camp at Pietermaritzburg, on the eastern side of South Africa. After he had made two attempts to escape from the camp, the authorities suggested an 'arrangement of honour' whereby they would send him back to Blinkoog if he would promise not to venture far from home while the war was on. He gave his word.

As he entered the valley, he shouted for Yellow Boy. But there was no sign of the little man. For some time afterwards, Von Schauroth sought information that might explain his disappearance, but learned nothing. Probably Yellow Boy had been slaughtered when, three months before the surrender, first German troops, then South Africans, had passed through the valley - the Germans, the more hurried, lingering only long enough to commandeer the livestock, the South Africans staying a sufficient time to plunder the half-built Castle. Many of Von Schauroth's treasures were gone, and most of the furniture was damaged beyond repair; but the cache of jewels and gold coins was intact

No sooner had he started clearing up than some of the Hotten-tots returned, asking to be taken on again. He welcomed them, but explained that it would be many moons before he could afford to give them full rations. Undeterred, they scampered back to the jobs they had been doing two years before.

With some financial help from the Le Riche family, whom he visited a day or so after his return – chiefly, one may surmise, to set his mind at rest that Talita was still a spinster, was still keen on him – he bought sheep and cattle.

The financial help became a kind of dowry when, in February 1917, he and Talita were wed. He was forty-two; she was twenty-eight. By November of the following year, the month in which the armistice was signed, Talita had borne two children. No doubt Von Schauroth's pleasure from paternity would have been greater if one of his offspring had been a son. But still, the fact that he had not just one native-born child but two seems to explain why he was allowed to remain in the country, exceptional to the new admini-strators' rule that all German settlers who had fought in the war were to be repatriated.

Soon after learning of that dispensation, he must have won-dered whether his relief was misplaced. He received notification that his contract for the purchase of Blinkoog had been rescinded. The reason given – as translated from the Dutch by Talita; as fathomed from the bureaucratese by her father – was that not a single instalment had been paid for nearly five years. He travelled to Windhoek, where the district commissioner with whom he had negotiated the contract and to whom he had, unfailingly, paid the instalments was living in retirement. He tried to make sense of what the old man said: that, never mind the armistice, German victory was assured . . . every loyal soldier of the Fatherland would be rewarded . . . those in *German* South-West Africa could have whatever land they wanted, free of charge – so, was not the Baron tickled pink, now that he understood that not a pfennig of the money he had paid in since August 1914 had been wasted but was safe and sound in a bank account in his name . . .?

His head still reeling, Von Schauroth went to the bank and withdrew the thousands of marks. The inflation raging in Ger-many had made them almost valueless.

During the next several months, he was forced to grovel to officials in the Department of Land – who at last, having run out of excuses for prolonging his agony, agreed to reinstate the contract. There were two conditions, however, the first being that the outstanding instalments were to be based on the pre-war value of the mark, the second being that the full amount had to be paid by the summer of 1922, about three years away.

Since he had no hope of retaining Blinkoog if he stayed there, working the land, Von Schauroth applied for a job with the Consolidated Diamond Mines, one of the few large and expanding concerns in the country, saying that he was prepared to be sent anywhere. Taking him at his word, the company offered him a position as an overseer of black workers at a prospecting camp near the centre of the arid coastal strip to the south of Walvis Bay. Leaving Talita and his daughters at Blinkoog, he became a paid prisoner in the Forbidden Area – so called because of the stringent security measures enforced by armed members of the Diamond Police. No one without a permit could enter the area; hours before a worker was allowed out, he had to take a dose of castor-oil so as to ensure that by the time he arrived at a borderpost, there to undergo a thorough search, any diamonds he had swallowed or prodded into his anus had been evacuated. There was no need for precautions against trespass from the sea, for rip-tides swirling between jagged rocks made it almost impossible to reach the shore, and anyone managing to survive was faced with a further barrier of vast tracts of shifting sands.

On behalf of Blinkoog, Von Schauroth would remain in the Forbidden Area for eight years. When the date for the settlement of the debt came close, he handed over all of his savings to the Department of Land and took out a mortgage bond for the amount that was then outstanding. There is no indication whether it was his idea or Talita's, but after leasing the valley to a sheep-farmer on a season-by-season basis, she, with the children, joined Von Schauroth at the camp, where he had rented married quarters. She added to their income by teaching music and embroidery to other white wives and their daughters in the enclosed community.

In November 1924, she gave birth to a boy. Von Schauroth was delighted – and, perhaps, relieved, for he was now fifty – at having a son and heir. Writing to relatives in Germany, he spoke of 'the little Baron'. Although the boy was christened Dietrich, after the most decorated of the generals in the Von Schauroth line, he was always called Dieter.

Three years later, Von Schauroth gave in his notice and took his family back to Blinkoog. During the time he had been away, he had dreamed of completing the Castle; had drawn plans for a top floor, stretching back beyond the shelf in the hillock, and for a square, crenellated tower at a front corner of the structure and rising high above it. As soon as the Hottentots, some now with sons, reappeared, he set most of them to work at cutting sandstone in aid of his dream.

But the natives were not the only people who had noticed his return. When he went to Karasburg to buy building materials, he was handed a letter from a leader of the *Deutsche Bund*, an organisation that had been set up to look after the interests of the German settlers, inviting him to become its director-general. An excellent salary was offered; also a house, close to the *Bund*'s headquarters – which were in the capital, Windhoek.

Von Schauroth was in two minds about the invitation. He hated the idea of leaving his beloved valley, from which he had been away for so long – of delaying the completion of the Castle – but was he not duty-bound to serve his countrymen? The answer, he decided, was yes. He had no choice. Maybe he talked things over with Talita before writing a letter of acceptance.

A few months after the move to Windhoek, a second son was born. He was called Udo.

Von Schauroth headed the *Deutsche Bund* until 1935, when he resigned rather than carry out the orders of the executive committee, most of the members of which were active supporters of the National Socialist Party in Germany, some numbering among their activities assaults on Jewish settlers. The day before he went back to Blinkoog, he told reporters: 'I will not do Hitler's dirty work.' His stand against the Nazis earned him the admiration of other opponents of them; the most useful expression of the admiration was the loan to him of breeding sheep, but what pleased him more was the return of his sword of honour by the ex-soldier who had stolen it.

From now on, for the rest of his life, he devoted himself to Blinkoog. At first, he *used* his obsession with the significances of the valley to save himself from thinking of what was happening in his country, to his countrymen; but soon, usage of the obsession had made it so powerful that the valley was all that mattered to him. No doctor would have certified him insane, but that is only because medical definitions of insanity are almost as insufficient as are legal ones. He permitted himself no rest during projects, and since one project followed another without a break, he never rested; any pleasure he derived from achievement of a goal was diminished by concerns about the following task, pre-planning of the one after. Work on the completion of the Castle came first, but while it was in progress, he decided to level part of the top of the hillock so that the ground floor could be extended; as soon as the flat roof was on and the tower built, the Hottentots were put to making a wide verandah – and already Von Schauroth was thinking of creating a U-shaped wing, enclosing a courtyard with fountains. Out-houses and workers' cottages went up . . . a perimeter-fence was erected . . . pens were made for the sheep, the meat and fur from which paid for the purchased materials . . . the valley was criss-crossed with dirt-roads, and a wider road was made, sweeping from steps in the side of the hillock to an imposing gate in the fence . . . orchards and a large flower-garden were planted.

One of the few social visitors to the Castle recalls that Von Schauroth was 'strict to an unusual degree with himself, his servants, and his family. When he came in to breakfast, he expected his sons to stand to attention while he looked to see if they were properly groomed, and then he would nod to them to be seated.'

Physically, the sons were markedly unlike. Udo, the younger, resembled his father, being tall, blond, and blue-eyed; Dieter, who had his mother's brown eyes and dark, wavy hair, only grew to five feet six, and slight rotundness and a tendency to slouch gave the impression that he was even shorter.

They were dissimilar in other ways.

Udo had a good brain, was manually dextrous, and excelled at sports. He did well at the boarding school which he and his brother attended, and went on to university. Having taken a degree as Bachelor of Science, he joined a firm of surveyors in Cape Town to gain experience, and then set up on his own in Karasburg – with such success that he was soon able to buy a farm and, after marrying a girl of good family whom he had met at university, to build a large house in the village.

Dieter was always near the bottom of his class. He was a duffer at games. His pride at being a Von Schauroth was sometimes manifested as arrogance, which may explain why, despite being amusing and generous, he made few friends. Leaving school when he was sixteen, he worked at Blinkoog before being sent by his father to a model estate owned by a rich farmer who had been chairman of the *Deutsche Bund* until that organisation was infiltrated by Nazis, and who had offered to teach Dieter modern methods of farming, with special reference to the breeding of caracul sheep. Upon his return, he spoke excitedly of putting what he had learned into effect.

But his enthusiasm soon waned – partly, it seems, because his desire to please his father was overtaken by fear of failure. Arguments between the Baron and Dieter increased in frequency, became more heated; during one of the rows, the old man shouted that the great sorrow in his life was that Udo, a true aristocrat, was not his first son – that the thought of Dieter's succeeding to the baronetcy appalled him. Dieter packed his bags and travelled to a town on the far side of the Great Karas Mountains, where he got a job as a skin-buyer. It was soon apparent to his employer, and expensively so, that Dieter had overstated his qualifications. The employer felt that he had been put in an awkward position, for he transacted much business with the Baron, and did not want to risk offending him by firing his son; as a way out of the dilemma, he arranged for a skin-trading company at Windhoek to offer Dieter an apprenticeship, and told him that the opportunity was far too good to turn down. Playing along with the ruse, Dieter gave in his notice. He went back to Blinkoog.

The Baron gave in to Talita's pleas that he should pretend to believe Dieter's unbelievable explanation for why he had become unemployed. Dieter, who had dreaded inquisition by and hostility from his father, did his best not to say or do anything that might mar the pleasant atmosphere. In particular, he raised no objection, as he had in the past, when his father put forward the idea that he should continue his education.

Arrangements were made for him to go to a well-regarded cramming school in Cape Town, starting at the end of 1948. Just before he set off on the five-hundred-mile journey south, his father, unable to express his hopes in words, handed him a ring with the family crest cut in black stone.

At twenty-four, he was the oldest pupil at the school. Years later, the wife of the principal recalled that, when he arrived, he was 'absolutely petrified'. She and her husband 'tried to make him feel at home and encouraged the other boys to befriend him. In spite of all our efforts, he never made friends. I never saw him speaking to any of the girls in his class. He was a moody sort of person and always struck me as a dreamer who lived in another world. But he was always neatly dressed and took a pride in his appearance, and he used to wear a ring which he seemed to pride.'

In the spring of 1950, he failed a university-entrance examination, but shortly afterwards gained certificates in German and mathematics. Leaving the school, he got a job as a junior clerk with an insurance company in Johannesburg.

Within a few months, he took lodgings in an expensive suburb – mystifyingly to his colleagues, unable to fathom how he could afford such luxury on a salary of little more than £400 a year. The mystery was brought to the notice of the office-manager, who, having made discreet enquiries revealing that Dieter was not getting funds from his father, suggested to him that he was spending beyond his means. In a tone of stealthy boastfulness, Dieter said that he was living on as well as in the house – his rent foregone by the landlady, with whom he was having an affair, and his meals provided by her daughter, with whom he was more greatly enjoying a similarly close relationship. Doubt was cast on the story during the following year, when it came to light that, from soon after his recruitment, he had been using a 'front company' to buy policies from working-class people who were in arrears with premiums, and to pay the premiums until the policies had a surrender-value. There was nothing criminal about the scheme, but he was dismissed from his job because he had obtained the names and addresses of likely policy-sellers from the insurance company's records.

He returned to South-West Africa, and spent the next four years working for one skin-buying firm after another, staying with none for long. A manager of the Windhoek Central Co-operative, which put up with him for eighteen months, afterwards explained: 'We had hoped that the name of Von Schauroth, associated with our firm, would be good for us. But Dieter was inefficient, lazy, unwilling to improve himself. I often felt like giving him a good shaking to wake him up.' And a fellow-worker at the Co-operative recalled that Dieter 'wanted to get rich overnight without having to work for it. He seemed to be more interested in minerals and semi-precious stones than in the pelts of his trade. Often, when he went out to the farms, he would return with a mere 400 skins – but also with 200 stones that might be worth, say, £10 in all, if that. He showed me rubbish which he treasured as if it was full of gold or some other valuable minerals.'

By the autumn of 1955, Dieter was back at Blinkoog. His father, now eighty-one, was still full of plans for the valley; but he had become frail of form, and was soon exhausted by even slight physical effort. He at first resisted Talita's entreaties that he should give their wayward son a responsible job, but then acceded, saying that Dieter could take charge of the by-now large flock of caracul sheep.

For the first time in his life, Dieter did something well. At the start, the Hottentot foreman told by the Baron to keep an eye on his son reported that he had an amazing knowledge of caraculs. Before long, that knowledge was shown to be not just theoretical: Dieter's pairing of ewes and rams produced strains of excellent quality; caraculs that he had bought at auction, many at knock-down prices, enhanced the flock.

He gloried in his success – but soon felt impelled to celebrate it in drink. More and more often, he spent evenings and his days off in the saloon at Karasburg. Despite the increasing frequency of the outings, he increased the number of bottles he stowed in the estate-car before driving back to the Castle. His drinking may not have affected his work; but his father's expressions of concern that it was or would were taken by him to be indicative of the fact that the old man either underrated his success or considered it to be fragile – and that, harming his confidence, caused a deterioration in his work, later aggravated by his father's criticisms.

In the autumn of 1957, the Baron made a new will. The terms of the one it replaced are not known.

Six months later, on a day at the end of March, he fell asleep while putting finishing touches to a sketch-plan for an ancillary reservoir, and did not awaken. He was buried beside the first orchard he had planted in the valley. The grave was marked with a slab of sandstone taken from a pile that he had meant to use to enlarge the Castle, and was called 'the Baron's little castle' by the Hottentots.

Much of the money he left went to Talita and his daughters, both of whom were now married and living in South Africa. The valley was split in two, the part including the Castle going to Udo, the rest to Dieter. By that division, the Baron had signified his sureness that the family honour was safer with his younger son – or, put as Dieter must have thought when the will was read, that the first son was so unworthy of succeeding to the baronetcy that there was ample justification for depriving him of the baronial domain. If either brother wished to sell his land, he had to offer it within the family, at a nominal price of about £1 for every 2½ acres, before accepting a bid from an outsider. Conditional upon each of the brothers agreeing to pay Talita £50 a month for the rest of her life, they each received half of the moveable assets of Blinkoog and the money that remained after cash bequests had been paid.

Under one of the terms of the will, if Udo paid Dieter half of some £6000 he owed the estate on a mortgage maturing in the summer of 1962, the debt would be settled. Dieter accepted Udo's offer to fence part of his land for him and to make out a cheque post-dated to 3 July 1962 for the balance of £1150.

That cheque would be a direct cause of one man's sudden death; an indirect cause of the sudden death of another.

Baron Dieter von Schauroth tried to hide his disappointment, his embarrassment, that he had not inherited the Castle. Perhaps that was one of the reasons why he spent more time in the saloon at Karasburg, drank more heavily, included more strangers in the rounds he bought. Perhaps it was one of the reasons why he exaggerated the worth of his father's legacy to him. Perhaps it was one of the reasons why he spoke of great plans he had for making money – of becoming the richest and most famous of all the Von Schauroths.

For a few months, both he and his mother continued to live at the Castle – by courtesy of Udo, who had said that they could stay there for as long as they liked, since he had no intention of moving from his house at Karasburg. But then Talita decided to join one of her daughters. The Castle became more of a base than a home to Dieter, who, leaving the Hottentots to look after his sheep and other livestock, was often away from the valley for days on end, sometimes – so he told drinking companions – travelling hundreds of miles for 'business meets'. A new Ford Galaxie car, coloured fire-engine red, was the most apparent of his several extravagances, all bought with the aid of loans that he had promised to repay, or start repaying, as soon as probate was granted on his father's will.

His efforts to impress succeeded only with the easily impressionable. A businessman who met him about this time afterwards recalled that 'although he always had in his pocket a fairly large sum of money, which he was fond of flashing, I soon reviewed my opinion of him. When I got to know him better, I realised that although he wanted to act the wealthy playboy, he didn't have enough money to play the part.' So delighted was he with his performance that he couldn't resist revealing the secret of his main 'prop' to certain people whom he felt he had no need to deceive. A garage mechanic in Karasburg, for instance: 'He took a large roll of notes from his pocket. I was surprised to see him carry so much money, and asked how many thousand pounds he had there. He laughed and said, "It shows how easily I can fool you people." He then showed me that he had made a large roll from bits of paper and had wrapped two £5 notes around it to make it look as if he had a lot of money on him.'

When an insurance agent in Karasburg tried to sell him a life policy, he said that he had better uses for his money, adding that he begrudged paying £53 a year on a policy that his father had taken out for him. Soon afterwards, in the saloon at Karasburg, he got talking with two commerical travellers, strangers to him and to each other, and having directed the conversation towards ways of making easy money, expressed interest when one of the men referred to a newspaper report concerning a person who had attempted to defraud an insurance company by faking death from drowning; and more interest still when the other traveller mentioned a poem, *The Ballad of Steinherz*, which told the true story of an impoverished merchant of Kecskemet, in Hungary, who took out life insurance and arranged his own murder so that his wife might become a wealthy widow.

That Dieter was prepared – or believed that he was prepared – to go to almost any lengths to acquire riches seems to be indicated by a plan that he thought up, and then discussed with a friend, to circumvent the family-first restriction on the sale of his land: if he married someone (anyone would do), he could at once adopt a child – and at once pretend to sell the land to the child at the nominal price – and at once sell the land on the open market. The friend pointed out some snags that to him, though not to Dieter, were obvious, and Dieter eventually agreed that the plan was impracticable.

A sequence of events subsequent to that discussion was almost certainly coincidental to it. In January 1959, Dieter drove to Cape Town for a holiday. At a suburban night-club called the Comet, he persuaded the manager to introduce him to a party of revellers, treated them to dinner, champagne and brandy, and then danced and chatted with the youngest of them, a pretty and well-built seventeen-year-old girl named Colleen Cairns, until closing time, when he paid the bill, over-tipped the waiters, and escorted Colleen to her home in a slum quarter of the city. She by then knew that he was a baron, and understood that he was extremely wealthy. He had learned that she was the fifth of nine children, the four youngest of whom were being brought up in institutions because the father, a man of mixed Irish and South African descent who was a line inspector on the State Railways, had deserted his family shortly before its completion, and that Colleen, having left school the year before and worked for a while in a shoe factory, was now employed as a telephonist and two-finger typist in a jewellery shop, at a salary of £10 a month. By the time Dieter said good-night, it was agreed that he would return to the dilapidated house within a few hours and take Colleen for a holiday on his farm.

Their departure was delayed because alterations had to be made to five dresses of the new wardrobe he insisted on buying for her. As soon as they arrived at the hotel in Karasburg, he arranged to show off Colleen at a dinner-party to which he invited all of his regular drinking companions and their wives or girl-friends. Next day, he showed off the valley to Colleen. He may have told her that only half of the land was his; that the Castle belonged to his younger brother. She afterwards remembered that he took her into every room and, pausing by each of the paintings of his ancestors, outlined the history of the Von Schauroths, ending with the words, 'I am the black sheep of the family,' spoken so seriously that she assumed that he was joking.

A week or so later, during one of their visits to Karasburg, a man and a woman – both 'distinguished-looking,' Colleen thought – passed them, giving Dieter a slight nod. Colleen asked who they were, and Dieter said that they were his brother and sister-in-law – no more than that. After a month – the happiest of Colleen's life; probably of Dieter's, too – Udo invited them to dinner at his house. It appears that Udo and his wife tried so hard to put Colleen at ease that she was crippled by shyness, hardly able to speak for fear of making a social gaffe, eating practically nothing rather than risk using the wrong cutlery. Back at the Castle, she broke down in tears. If Dieter tried to comfort her, he did not succeed. The following morning, she still insisted upon leaving, and so he drove her home. They both believed that the affair was over.

But each of them needed the other, though in a different way; and when, after a fortnight, Dieter telephoned Colleen, asking her to return, she did not have to be persuaded to board the next bus to Karasburg. If, upon arrival, she enquired how he had got a graze on his head, he probably did not tell her the truth: that, while waiting for her at the hotel, he had discussed with a visitor ways of acquiring illicit diamonds, and then, having gathered that the man had diamonds hidden in his truck, wrenched open the door of the cab – only to be made aware, forcibly by a blow struck with a spanner, that the man's coloured servant used the truck as sleeping quarters.

Colleen had been back at the Castle for a month when Talita arrived. After some initial embarrassment – for although Dieter had known that his mother was coming, he had not thought to tell her that he had company – the two women, one seventeen, the other seventy, got on well together: so well that, before long, they were telling each other things that Dieter would have preferred them to keep to their respective selves. Colleen was too recently pregnant to be sure that she was in that condition, and so perhaps something she said about the reckless nature of Dieter's love-making, indicating that it was almost bound to be productive, caused Talita to speak sternly, even threateningly, to her son. Straightway after the interview, Dieter asked Colleen to marry him. She said yes.

The marriage was performed by a magistrate in Cape Town on 21 May 1959: exactly eight months before Colleen gave birth to a boy. During those months, Dieter was busy, though rarely industrious. For most of the time, he and Colleen lived at the Castle. Before her pregnancy became visibly apparent, he sent her back to Cape Town for a six weeks' course at a charm school. Whatever the cost of the tuition, he had difficulty in raising it. The money he had received from his father's will had gone to clear some of his debts and to pay the interest on some others; most of the regular but variable income he derived from the slaughter of sheep was needed to settle bills that were so long overdue that the creditors were threatening legal action, refusing to accept further orders, or both. Adding to his worries, there was a serious drought: grazing land for the sheep was diminishing as stretches of the valley became too dry even to sustain grass.

Most men in his situation would have made economies in their social expenditure. Not Dieter. He continued to drink heavily, to buy large rounds; whenever he and Colleen went to Cape Town, he booked into a five-star hotel and took her, and others, to the best restaurants; he bought her jewellery and fine gowns. And, in December, when his bank overdraft was at the limit imposed by the manager, he approached the insurance agent who, a year before, he had turned away: he had decided, he said, to take out not one but two policies on his life, each for £10,000. While the agent was making the arrangements, Dieter wrote to a friend who had become an insurance broker in Cape Town: 'Please get the necessary forms from all insurance companies doing life business in South Africa. I want to give each company a £3000 whole-life non-profit policy. My next birthday is on November 30, when I will be thirty-six. . . . Also please find out about your commission, as I want half, because I don't like to see so much money wasted. . . . Money is rolling in now. . . .'

Replying, the friend said, among other things, that if Dieter took out policies with all thirty-one companies doing life-insurance business, the annual premiums would amount to £1860.

On 20 January 1960, the day before his son was born, Dieter wrote back: 'You cannot frighten me with big premiums. I am glad to hear that you do not mind splitting the commissions in equal proportion. That just gives me a kick, and I feel like having earned that money, and it will give me great pleasure to spend it some-how. . . . Get together all the necessary forms.'

In March and April, he sold most of his sheep and some farm equipment for about £7000. Having paid off almost all of his overdraft, he was left with about £5000, which he kept in cash. At the beginning of May, he arranged for the rest of the sheep and equipment to be sold, and then, with Colleen and the baby, set off for Cape Town in the new Galaxie car that he was buying on hire-purchase. He had told friends in Karasburg that he would be returning to the valley, to start farming again, once the drought was over. None of them believed him.

A day or so later, he visited the insurance broker at his office in the centre of Cape Town. Corresponding with him over the past month, he had gradually changed his mind about the number of life policies he wished to take out – also, though only slightly, about the total of both the annual premiums and the settlement amounts. Now he signed five proposals for policies totalling £110,000, on which the premiums would be just over £1900. Directly afterwards, he called on a friend at the Standard Bank. Trying rather too hard to appear casual, he ripped open a brown-paper parcel, emptied its contents of wads of currency notes on to the man's desk, and told him to count out two piles, one of £2000, to be deposited in a savings account, the other of £1900, for transfer to the insurance broker. That having been done, he stuffed the remaining notes, worth about £1300, in his pockets.

By October, that ready cash had been spent, only a few pounds remained in the savings account, and the little that was left of the £3600 realised by the sale of the last of the moveable assets of his land was considerably short of what he owed to sundry creditors. Close to £1500 had gone to furnish the flat that he was renting in a modern block in a smart section of the city; much more had been lost to bookmakers at two race-courses he frequented. Attempts have been made to give an exact accounting of his incomings and outgoings, but none can be relied upon: if for no other reason than because, although it is known that he had dealings with several petty peddlers of illicit diamonds, there is no way of knowing whether, let alone by how much, he profited or lost from the shady transactions.

Early in November, he arranged for yet more life insurance: a short-term policy covering him for £70,000 for six months, at a single premium of £154. The broker again agreed to share his commission – then, changing the subject from insurance to investment, spoke of a proposal to start a chain of roadhouses and motels. Without thinking twice, Dieter said that he would put £20,000 into the scheme. He agreed to sign a part-cession of his new policy in favour of a company controlled by the broker.

The policy was issued on 17 November.

Next day, Dieter made a will.

His working out of the bequests was based on a reckoning of what would be left of a total insurance settlement of £201,000 after payment of his debts and of death duties. As well as leaving his part of Blinkoog to his son, he gave instructions for the setting up of a trust-fund to provide for the boy's maintenance and education and to pay him a lump-sum when he was grown up. A similar fund was to be set up for the second child that Colleen was expecting. Cash bequests were to go to Colleen, his mother, and his sisters and brother.

Of course, Dieter's testamentary arithmetic would need to be revised should he fail to keep any of the nine life policies in force – most drastically if, in six months' time, he was unable to renew the short-term policy for £70,000.

Dieter first met Marthinus Rossouw in the middle of January 1961. They were introduced by a mutual acquaintance who, knowing that Dieter was ever eager to acquire illicit diamonds and that Marthinus was acting as 'contact-man' for some black diggers who claimed to have stones for sale, believed that they – and he – might profit from the encounter. Though the deal that the two men arranged fell through, each was much impressed by the other. 'As soon as I saw Dieter,' Marthinus afterwards recalled, 'I knew that he was a man of standing.' Returning from an abortive tryst with the diggers, Dieter let Marthinus drive his car – and looked on admiringly when Marthinus, irritated by the behaviour of another road-user, overtook the offending vehicle and forced it on to a verge. 'You're a real cowboy,' he said. 'One of these days I must get you to shoot someone for me.'

The 23-year-old Marthinus didn't take the second part of the congratulatory comment seriously, but he was delighted to be called a real cowboy. That was the greatest praise he had ever received. Since childhood, he had aped the heroes of Hollywood movies about the Wild West: as soon as it was possible, he had grown a thin moustache, just like Robert Taylor's; as soon as he was earning money as a signal-fitter on the State Railways, he had taken to wearing broad-brimmed hats, checked shirts, levis shrunken to show off his slim legs, riding boots that added a couple of inches to his natural tallness – and had bought a guitar and, somewhat aided by a correspondence course, learnt to strum from it the home-on-the-range sort of tunes of Gene Autry and Roy Rogers. Often, when he arrived late for work, he explained that his plane from Texas had been delayed; and his workmates almost came to accept the reason he gave for disappearing at meal-times, which was that he needed to mosey down to a corral in the railway yard, just to make sure that his pony hadn't been rustled. Of his several tattoos, the most complicated, on his right forearm, consisted of the word *LOVE*, a dagger, a half-moon, and the name *Johanna Dynamite*. It commemorated a night in 1956 when he had 'won' an eighteen-year-old girl called Johanna from 'The Killers', a gang of young tearaways in the Salt River district of Cape Town, who considered her their property. Some time afterwards, Johanna had attested to her vow, 'I belong to you now,' by marrying Marthinus. They and the children Johanna had borne were now living in what to Marthinus was 'a little old log-cabin in the west': actually, a shanty of corrugated iron in a railway siding.

It would seem that the classified advertisements in South African newspapers are more worthy of study by the criminally inclined than are those in British ones. A couple of days after the first meeting between Dieter and Marthinus, the *Cape Argus* carried an advertisement offering a Beretta automatic pistol, 'as new', together with three boxes of ammunition, for £10. Dieter bought the goods – perplexingly to Colleen, who reminded him, without getting a response, that he already owned a hand-gun.

There is no evidence that he displayed the Beretta to Marthinus – not at that time, that is. But as their friendship grew – until, within a fortnight, they were seeing each other almost every night – Dieter spoke much of firearms. Once, when they were in a bar, Dieter insisting that all the drinks were on him, he suggested that Marthinus should become his bodyguard, and then asked: 'Can you shoot?'

'I certainly can,' the young man replied, perhaps slightly upset that his reputation as the fastest draw this side of Laramie was not known to Dieter, the dude-rancher. 'On my uncle's farm, I could hit a penny with a rifle at a hundred yards.'

Dieter repeated, almost word for word, what he had said during their first excursion about getting Marthinus to shoot someone for him. And added: 'I'll pay you £5000.'

'Bring me the guy,' Marthinus said, entering into the joke.

On a subsequent occasion, Dieter told Marthinus that the most efficient – and most humane – way of killing someone was to fire a bullet into the back of the neck. 'That way they don't feel a thing,' he said. 'When you shoot that man for me, put two shots in, to make sure, and you'll get your £5000.'

Marthinus told, first, Johanna, then his mother, about the conversations. Both advised him to steer clear of Dieter, but he took no notice.

Early in February, Colleen was rushed to hospital, suffering from severe labour pains. The child, delivered prematurely, was dead.

Dieter did not amend his will. His mind was too taken up with worries about how he was to meet the insurance premiums that were starting to fall due. After somehow managing to pay the first of them, he was only able to pay another – on the last day allowed – by arranging for an acquaintance to 'steal' his Galaxie, then haggling with the motor-insurance company on the basis that if they wrote out a cheque more promptly than was their custom, it could be for an amount far below that for which the car was covered.

On the last day of February, Marthinus showed Dieter a letter that he had received from his employers, informing him that he was being transferred to the railway workshops at Kromrivier, more than 300 miles from Cape Town, on 27 March.

Dieter looked dismayed. 'What will I do if I still want you to shoot that man for me?' he asked quietly.

Laughing, Marthinus said, 'Bring him to me at Kromrivier!'

As soon as Dieter arrived home, he wrote a note:

I, the undersigned, hereby give to Marthinus Rossouw cheque No. CA 11 358158, post-dated to 3rd July 1962, signed by Udo von Schauroth, for the sum of £1150, which my brother owes me. I give it to him for services rendered.

D. VON SCHAUROTH

On the evening of Thursday, 23 March, Marthinus told Dieter that he had only been able to scrape up half of £40 he needed as a deposit on an old car he wanted to buy, and Dieter said that he would given him £20 the next day. At the end of the evening, after Dieter had driven Marthinus home in a car that he had borrowed from one of his sisters, he handed him an envelope, saying, 'There's a post-dated cheque for you in there, and if in the meantime you need money, let me know. When you shoot that man for me, you'll get £5000.'

He had driven off by the time Marthinus tore open the envelope and stared at the cheque, at the note to which it was pinned. 'For services rendered. . . .' *What* services? Marthinus was bewildered. Was the cheque genuine? Did Dieter mean what he had written? Or were the slips of paper additions to his idea of a joke?

On Friday morning, Dieter took off the ring his father had given him twelve years before, and put it in a safe place.

He took Colleen to a restaurant for lunch. She noticed that he was more cheerful than he had been for months. In the afternoon, they made love, then went to sleep.

Wakening at five o'clock, he jumped out of bed, telling Colleen, 'It's late. I have an appointment. Big business.' He hurriedly pulled on a yellow and white checked shirt, green corduroy trousers, bright-coloured socks, reddish-brown shoes, and a brown corduroy jacket, and left the flat.

It was six when he met Marthinus below the clock in the main railway station. He gave him the £20 he had promised, then drove him to see the man who was selling him the old car. Marthinus told the man that he would soon be able to afford a far more expensive car, and displayed the post-dated cheque and the note assigning it to him. After arranging to return on Monday afternoon, he rejoined Dieter.

They drove to the Prince of Wales Hotel. Still sitting in Dieter's borrowed car, they had a brief discussion, during which Dieter handed Marthinus money for drinks; then they entered the bar of the hotel separately, each ordered a drink (Dieter had a whisky and soda; Marthinus made himself memorable to the barman by asking for brandy to be polluted with Coca-Cola), and pretended to be complete strangers who were merely passing the time of day.

But when the barman was out of earshot, Dieter offered a toast: 'Here's to Kromrivier.'

'I'm sorry I'm going,' Marthinus said. 'I can't stay late. I told Johanna I'd be back by nine to help with the packing.'

'All right, cowboy,' Dieter said – 'but before you go, you must do that job for me.'

'Tonight?'

'Yes.'

Dieter left first; Marthinus followed a minute later.

They went through the same pretending-to-be-strangers act at the Cambridge Hotel in Milnerton, ten miles north of Cape Town. Marthinus had never been in the bar before, but Dieter had often drunk there after attending race-meetings at the Ascot course, just outside the town. The act was made harder to sustain by the intervention of an off-duty detective of the private sort, a man named Jacob Beyleveld; feeling lonely, he latched on to the two men who appeared to have just met. Marthinus, jittery for a reason he could not explain to the unwelcome third-party, kept leaving the room – so frequently that Beyleveld eventually asked Dieter, 'What's wrong with that chap? He's in and out like a jack-in-the-box.'

Having left the Cambridge, one after the other, Dieter and Marthinus drove a few miles farther on, to the Killarney Hotel, where they briefly performed the act, and then – Marthinus now at the wheel, Dieter giving directions – continued north towards the town of Malmesbury.

Dieter sang German marching-songs that he had learnt from his father.

Marthinus was silent.

They had travelled six miles from the Killarney when Dieter told Marthinus to slow down – then to drive into a clearing bounded by thick bush and eucalyptus trees. Once they were parked, Dieter pulled his raincoat from the back of the car. After wrapping a piece of cloth round his hand, he withdrew the Beretta and two boxes of cartridges from a pocket of the raincoat, slipped two cartridges into the pistol, and gave it to Marthinus.

They got out of the car. The moon, full that night, was strong enough to make their shadows distinct on the sandy ground. Seeing Dieter gazing intently at the eucalyptus, Marthinus pointed the pistol in the same direction, half-expecting to see a person emerge from between the trees.

I have taken his word for some details of some of the incidents leading up to this moment. Now – *so he afterwards said* – Dieter spoke his name, and the following conversation took place.

'Yes?' he whispered back.

'Here is the man you have to shoot. *I* am the man.'

Marthinus did not reply.

'I want you to shoot me,' Dieter said.

'Don't be ridiculous.'

'I told you. I'm tired of living, and I'm unhappy with my wife. I can't shoot myself, because then they won't pay out the insurance. As I promised, you'll get £5000. Go to my bank manager, and he'll give you the money.'

'What are you saying, Dieter? Forget it. You can't be serious.'

'I am. No one will ever know. Kill me. Drive the car to Milnerton. Leave it there. Take a bus back to town. Throw the pistol and cartridges into the sea. Don't talk to anyone.'

'It's ridiculous.'

'Aren't you my friend?'

'The best friend I ever had – the only friend. How can I do this to you?'

'I won't even feel it. I'll be dead with the first shot – unconscious. Fire twice to make sure.'

Dieter turned away. '*Here*,' he said, touching the back of his neck.

Before seven o'clock next morning, a labourer, cycling to work, saw the body of a man lying in the clearing, about seventy yards from the road. He waved down a motorist, who, after looking at the body from a distance, said that the police should be informed. Either the labourer or the motorist was an unreliable eyewitness, for whereas the former subsequently stated that the body was lying face upwards, the latter was sure that it was lying on its stomach. The motorist added that 'the right arm stretched backwards, and the palm of the hand was upwards. I think the left arm lay slightly under the body. The legs were straight and slightly apart.'

But for apartheid, the question of which of the men was right would probably not have arisen. The first policemen to arrive at the scene were a uniformed constable, youthful and inexperienced, and a detective, who happened to be black. Because of his colour, the detective stood by, waiting to be told what to do by his white superior. The constable pottered around the body, unconcernedly scuffing the ground, before moving the body about (to such effect that photographs that were eventually taken showed a pool of blood some distance from the two bullet-wounds in the base of the skull) and searching the pockets (all but one of which were empty: the fob-pocket of the green corduroy trousers contained the sum of £2.12.6d.). The constable found a cartridge-shell near the feet of the corpse – but whether the feet had been that near to the shell, nearer still, or farther away, before the constable's rummaging, is a moot point. After ordering the detective to stand guard – and not, repeat not, touch anything – he returned to his station in the town of Philadelphia, and from there telephoned police headquarters in Cape Town.

The white detective who arrived within half an hour noted that the ground in the vicinity of the body showed no sign that a struggle had taken place; that none of the pockets had been turned out (of course, the constable may have found one or more turned out – and, keen for commendation as a tidy searcher, turned them in); that the man's wrist-watch had stopped at 9.10 (reports of the case give no indication whether or not the watch was examined by a clock-maker to see if it had stopped as the result of damage or simply needed winding); that an uncut diamond of less than five carats lay near the body (later, a few more uncut diamonds, none of much value, were found nearby).

The body remained unidentified till the afternoon. In the morning, the one of Dieter's sisters who had lent him her car travelled to the place in the centre of Cape Town where he had promised to leave it. There was no sign of the car. Though Colleen had telephoned her the night before to say that Dieter had not come home, the sister was more angry than worried. She returned to her farm. Later in the morning, she learnt from Colleen that Dieter was still missing. Soon afterwards, she heard on the radio that a man had been found shot dead near Milnerton, and straightway started making telephone calls – the last of which, to an officer at the police station at Philadelphia, convinced her that the dead man was her brother. She gave the officer details of her car. During the afternoon, it was found abandoned in Milnerton; a raincoat lay across the back seats.

The detective in charge of the case visited Colleen. An optimist, he showed her the uncut diamond that had been found in the clearing and asked if she recognised it. She didn't. But she said that her husband had had dealings in diamonds with several men, some of whom she named. 'He might have gone to meet one of them last night,' she said. 'He took £2000 with him.' Asked how she knew that Dieter had had that much cash, she said, 'He told me' – an answer that, in the light of subsequent inquiries, was shown to be evidentially worthless.

As a consequence of the interview with Colleen, Marthinus Rossouw was traced and taken in for questioning at police headquarters. He admitted having met Dieter at the railway station at six o'clock on the Friday evening – but said that they had parted no more than half an hour or so later, soon after he had paid a deposit of £40, half of it provided by Dieter, to a used-car salesman: then, so he said, he had picked up a girl and taken her to see a film called *Jack Slade* at the Rex Bioscope cinema; returning home at eleven, he had gone straight to bed.

Without even asking him the gist of *Jack Slade*, the investigators accepted his story, and allowed him to leave. However, on Monday morning they received a telephone call from Jacob Beyleveld, who, having seen a photograph of Baron Dieter von Schauroth in the *Cape Times*, was sure that he was one of two men he had met in the bar of the Cambridge Hotel at Milnerton about 7.30 on the Friday evening. Beyleveld's description of the other man – particularly of his cowboyesque attire – struck a chord with the detectives, and at three o'clock, when Marthinus arrived at the used-car lot, intending to collect his car and drive to Kromrivier, he was arrested and taken back to police headquarters. There, he was asked to repeat what he had said previously. Having done so, he was asked to read and then sign a written rendition of his story. And then he was put on an identification parade – at which, the police having done a pub-crawl in the past few hours, not only Jacob Beyleveld but barmen from the Cambridge and Killarney Hotels were photographed touching his shoulder recollectively. After that, he was lodged in a cell.

By eight o'clock, when he was returned to the interview room, he had concocted a new story. Quite forgetting that he and Dieter had been seen in the Killarney Hotel after their visit to the Cambridge, he said that when they had left the latter place, a gang of armed men had forced them to drive to the clearing, where, without preamble, one of the men had killed Dieter; directly after the shooting, he had been ordered to give another of the men a lift back to Milnerton; leaving the car in a side-street of the town, he had travelled home by public transport. He could not explain why he had not gone to the police.

'I don't believe you,' the senior detective said. 'You previously made two statements, one verbally and one in writing, which you now admit were full of lies. Why did you tell those lies?'

'I was afraid.'

'But if what you have now told us is true, what did you have to be afraid of?'

'Because I didn't think you would believe the truth.'

'Why not?'

'Well, because you wouldn't. You just *said* you don't believe it.'

Marthinus flushed with anger when the detective came straight out with the accusation that he had 'shot Von Schauroth to rob him'.

'If you think I robbed him,' he shouted, 'why do you think he gave me this?' And he produced from his pocket the post-dated cheque and the note.

That action was the prelude to a confession that he seemed almost grateful to the detective for believing. At midnight, he was escorted to the home of a magistrate – with whom, in accordance with South African law, he was left alone while he made a statement. Part of the transcription reads as follows:

> . . . I fired the first shot. Then I said, 'Goodbye, friend, we will see each other again.' Then I fired the second shot.
>
> At first I wanted to leave the car there. Then I decided to bring it to Milnerton, which I did. From there I took a bus home. After I arrived home, I said to my wife, 'I have shot Dieter dead.' She cried and I undressed and got into bed.
>
> I got up again, took the revolver and the cartridges and walked down to Cape Town, where I caught a Sea Point bus. I got off at the Ritz Hotel and walked over to the sea, where I threw the revolver away. . . .

Subsequently, Marthinus did two things which, between them, virtually erased any doubt of his guilt.

Taken to Sea Point, he indicated where he had thrown the Beretta (not a revolver but an automatic) and the boxes of cartridges. Some days later, a searching frogman located the weapon in a narrow opening between rocks on the sea-bed. Examination of it by a ballistics expert confirmed that it was the weapon that had fired the two bullets prised from Dieter's head during the autopsy.

In his cell, Marthinus wrote a long, self-pitying letter to Johanna. One sentence read: 'Your own husband has shot Dietrich von Schauroth, a baron of standing throughout South Africa.' He wrote on the back of the envelope, 'Remember the Friday evening of the 24th day of March 1961, your husband shot Baron Dietrich von Schauroth dead. Relieved him of his troubles.' At the end of a visit by Johanna, he slipped the letter into a book that she was taking away – but so clumsily that the action was observed by a warder, who confiscated the letter and passed it to the police.

The gun and the letter were made exhibits at the trial, which took place in September. Shortly before, the companies that had insured Dieter's life had agreed to guarantee some of the defence costs, on the understanding that Marthinus's counsel would be seeking to convince every member of the jury that the murder was committed, not at all in furtherance of robbery, but solely at the victim's request. Marthinus stood no chance of being acquitted, but he might escape execution – and the companies might resist claims from Dieter's estate – if the jury could be persuaded to add to the single-word verdict a recommendation for mercy, based on the extenuating circumstances of his crime.

Perhaps the jury were impressed by a pathologist's opinion that, within thirty minutes to a few hours after the murder, someone – Marthinus, while rifling the pockets? – had altered the position of the body. Perhaps they accepted Colleen's evidence that her husband was carrying £2000 when he left the flat. Perhaps they believed Jacob Beyleveld and the barman at the Cambridge Hotel, both of whom swore that they had noticed a bulge in Dieter's inside breast pocket. Or perhaps they simply reasoned that, whatever the instigation for the murder, Marthinus was most unlikely to have left the scene without searching the body for perks.

After the foreman of the jury had delivered the verdict of Guilty, he was asked by the registrar, 'Do you find that there are any extenuating circumstances?'

'We have been unable to find any,' he replied.

And so the judge did not need to qualify the sentence of death.

Owing chiefly to delays occasioned by unsuccessful petitionings, first for Marthinus to be allowed to appeal, and then for clemency, and by a commission of inquiry, instigated by the insurance companies, which found no fault with the verdict, the sentence was not carried out till 19 June 1962, only a fortnight short of when the post-dated cheque became payable. The cheque was Marthinus's sole tangible asset. In his will, made in the condemned cell, he left £500 of the £1150 to his father, who had spent all of his savings on the defence, and the remaining £650 to Johanna and his children. (His hope that Johanna would remarry was fulfilled within two months of his death.)

Although Udo must have known that the insurance companies' lawyers would construe his honouring of the cheque as an indication that he accepted that Dieter had assigned it to Marthinus as payment for his own murder, he did not arrange for it to be stopped.

Since the best-regarded of the companies that had insured Dieter for £10,000 had settled in full, the amount owed to the estate was £191,000. Knowledgeable persons writing for or to newspapers and business journals contended that, what with the jury's decision and the commission's finding, the creditor-companies could not advance the argument of 'constructive suicide' as a reason for withholding payment. None of the writers was allowed to say that the longer the companies held out, the more it would cost the estate in legal fees, and so the time would surely come when Dieter's executors felt that they had no choice but to accept a comparatively small payment, made *ex gratia*, without admission of liability, rather than incur further expense.

That time came exactly a year from the day when Marthinus was hanged. The payment was of £10,000. The companies agreed to reimburse the estate for costs incurred because of their delaying tactics.

By then, Colleen was working as a receptionist in the office of a newspaper that had published what was purported to be her life-story. Her son, the young Baron von Schauroth, was in the care of Talita. Udo was well advanced with plans to re-unite the two parts of the valley, his and his nephew's, and to furbish the Castle. Dieter's ashes had been scattered at Blinkoog; but, so far as I can tell, no one had thought to have a stone cut as a remembrance of him.

The Inconstant Wife

There are three recognised reasons why killers, having killed, decapitate their prey: farsightedly, to hinder identification of found remains; being inexpert at packing, to rearrange components of the corpse so that all fit snugly in a trunk; merely, or madly, because butchery seems a pleasurable perk of the enterprise. Only rarely does a killer have a sentimental reason, the desire for a keepsake, for beheading the victim.

Perhaps I am being charitable towards Michael Telling in saying that when he lopped off the head of his extremely late wife Monika (so late that her head must have been, among other blemishes, wizened, not unlike a prune), it was because he had dismissed, as being too impersonal, artefacts that less loving widowers might have considered apt as mementoes of matrimony. The fact that he couldn't bear to part with her head suggests that his love for all of her was blind and deaf (also, though only latterly, insensitive to smell), for, by most of many accounts, Monika was a thoroughly deserving victim.

Michael Telling is a member of the Vestey family, which is certainly among the least illustrious ennobled families in Great Britain, and probably among the three richest of all, aristocratic or common. He is a second cousin of the third Baron of Kingswood, Lord (Samuel) Vestey, who owes his title to the fact that in 1921, or thereabouts, his grandfather William paid £20,000 to the honours-broker Maundy Gregory, on the understanding that a Liberal share of that sum would go to the prime minister, David Lloyd George, who would, in return, make him, William Vestey, a baron. Lloyd George was not the first premier, nor the last, to profit from his powers of patronage; but only one of his successors has come close to him as a bestower of honours upon the dishonourable. A year or so before the Vestey transaction, Neville Chamberlain, who would himself become prime minister, wrote to a friend apropos of the latest Honours List: 'I have never ceased to congratulate myself that I did not figure in that rabble.' William Vestey (who had previously purchased a knighthood) was one of five men recommended for baronies in the King's Birthday Honours of 1922. Of that quintet, only a maker of custard powders was not suspected of having paid for his peerage. The worst of the remaining rogues was Sir Joseph Robinson, whose appeal against a conviction for fraud, carrying a fine of half a million pounds, had been dismissed as recently as November 1921. The second worst was Vestey. His citation asserted that he, as head of the Union Cold Storage Company, had 'rendered immense service' to the country by 'gratuitously' keeping perishable war supplies fresh in the company's storage depots at places on the Channel-coast of France. Actually, he had made immense profit from the 'service', for he had invoiced the British government for every cubic inch of chilled space provided. Far from helping the war effort, he had been a tax-dodger on a gigantic scale: so as to avoid paying income and excess-profits taxes, he had, in 1915, the first full year of the war, moved his meat-packing operations to Argentina, thereby throwing some five thousand of his compatriots out of work.

By the time he died, his lawyers and accountants and hirelings in the Inland Revenue had spun for him an intricate web of tax-avoidance schemes. Though not mentioned in his last will and testament, they were his most valuable legacy. During his son's life, the schemes were made almost immaculately unfathomable to civil servants whose curiosity was piqued in regard to how it was that the millions-a-year growth of the Vestey fortune was virtually unimpeded by deductions in aid of the Exchequer. In 1980, when 39-year-old Samuel Vestey was using the title bought by his grandfather, a journalist named Philip Knightley learnt more about the Vestey tax-dodges in a few months than the Inland Revenue had learnt over more than half a century. Mr Knightley reported the results of his investigation in October issues of the *Sunday Times*. While the series of articles was running, government spokesmen announced that some of the revealed loop-holes in the tax laws would be plugged. For all I know, some or all of the promised plugging has been done. It is sufficient to my purpose to quote only a few of Mr Knightley's sentences, those to do with one of the several companies belonging to the Vesteys:

Dewhurst the butchers has filed its results for 1979. In 1978 Dewhurst turned over £152,500,000, had a pre-tax profit of £2,300,000, and had paid just £10 in tax. Dewhurst has improved on this performance. Its 1979 turnover was £169,000,000, its pre-tax profit was £4,100,000. And its tax? Nil.

Such information – allegedly illustrative of how, at that time, any arithmeticians employed by the Vesteys to keep a running total of their wealth could treat the terms *gross* and *net* as being practically synonymous – may, about three years later, have come in handy to crime reporters who felt duty-bound to make a guess, give or take a few hundred millions, at the size of the fortune of the family that now included among its members a man accused of having murdered his wife.

Michael Henry Maxwell Telling was born – under the sign of Taurus: a fact that, even when he was grown up, was important to him – on 17 May 1950. If his mother (a grand-daughter of the first Lord Vestey) is to be believed, her husband, 'a violent and aggressive man with a drink problem', made her pregnancy uneasy by chasing her about the house with a cavalry sword. Though Michael was only three when his mother obtained a divorce and was granted custody of him, he seems to have inherited enjoyment in sword-play from the man he never saw again: by his ninth birthday, his mother, who had never shown much affection towards him, was deterred from showing any by what she termed his 'warnings off', which were accompanied by stabbing gestures with carving knives that he had either filched from the kitchen or bought with his excessive pocket-money. He 'embarrassed' her in many ways – for instance, by running naked from the house and lying down in the road; by breaking a bottle of full-cream milk over the head of a parson's daughter. He underwent treatment from psychiatrists at the Maudsley Hospital, in South London, and spent several terms at a school for maladjusted children; but neither experience was beneficial. At one unspecialising boarding school that he attended, he went into a diabetic coma after gorging himself on sweets that he had raided from the tuckshop; he was expelled from another in consequence of having stolen cash from fellow-pupils, and from another because he had set fire to a staircase. When he was sixteen, he sat O-Level examinations, and failed all of them.

That same year, his mother married an Australian diplomat. Soon afterwards, the newly-constituted family moved to Sydney. Like so many young people who are poorly educated, Michael was fascinated by electrical and mechanical gadgets; but unlike most of them, he did not need to save up to buy such things: if his allowance was ever insufficient, slight pestering of his mother caused her to add to it. His stepfather, whom he admired, persuaded him to attend a technical school, and he stayed there long enough, and behaved conscientiously enough, to gain passes in four single-subject examinations equivalent to English O-Levels. Then – though perhaps not in this order – he worked for two years, until being made redundant, on the shop-floor of a car factory; for six months, until being sacked, as a salesman in a men's clothing store; for six months, on and off, as a waiter in restaurants in towns along the south and south-west edges of Australia. The fact that he never worked for any of the Australian companies owned by the Vestey family may simply mean that, finding butchery and its kindred occupations unappealing, he preferred not to.

One restaurant wherein he waited at tables was in Perth. During his brief period of employment there, he was befriended by a waitress named Alison Webber, and when he moved on, she, at his pleading, accompanied him. Presumably there came a time, no later than the spring of 1976, when he took Alison to meet his mother – not only to announce his intention of returning with her to England and marrying her, but also, when she was out of earshot, to get advice on how to go about obtaining a marriage allowance from a Vestey trust-fund.

The arrangement made by the family's lawyers entitled him to £1200 a month (whether or not taxable, I cannot tell) and permitted him to receive reimbursement from the fund of all payments of credit-card accounts and in respect of running expenses of a Vestey grace-and-favour house in the South Devon seaside resort of Maidencombe, close to Torquay. It may be that there was a proviso to the arrangement, limiting both the number of his credit cards and the amount he could borrow on each of them; if not, he could have spent virtually without restraint.

The cliché, comforting to most of us, that money cannot buy happiness was true in the case of Michael and Alison Telling. Their marriage soon foundered. In March 1979, Alison gave birth to a son, called Matthew. Her hope that, as she put it, 'fatherhood

might give Michael a sense of purpose and make him less moody'
was not realised. He seemed only able to express his love for the
child in squandering ways: by acquiring all the paraphernalia of
home-movies (at the christening, he upset the officiating vicar by
his insistence on getting camera-angles just right), by wiring up
the house with an amplifying gadget that caused the slightest
sound from the cot to be relayed, deafeningly, to other rooms, and
by driving to London specially to find cuddly toys that, when
pressed, played lullabies. The child was a year old when Alison
instituted divorce proceedings. She afterwards described Michael
as 'a coward, unable to face his responsibilities'.

If he was grieved by the break-up of his marriage, he did not
show it. A new interest, in motor-cycles, occupied his mind. He
bought one machine after another, each more powerful, and in
October 1980, after seeing an advertisement in an enthusiasts'
magazine for a Harley-Davidson, the bike-equivalent of a Bentley,
flew 6000 miles to San Francisco, where the dealer dealt.

I should not be writing about him if he, having bought the
Harley-Davidson and arranged for its shipment, had not, on the
spur of the moment, decided to postpone his return to England: if
he had stayed at an hotel other than the St. Francis (the setting,
fifty-nine years before, of a wild party from which one of the
guests, a Hollywood bit-player named Virginia Rappe, never
recovered, consequently ruining the host, the film-star Fatty
Arbuckle, who was accused of having caused her death while
raping her): if, as he left the St. Francis on the first afternoon of his
overstaying, traffic-lights had not stopped him from crossing the
street. But for those *ifs*, and others, he would not have passed the
time of day with a union-negotiator named Louis Zumsteg and
his Swiss-born wife Elsa, who had just arrived in the city from their
home at Santa Rosa, fifty miles to the north. By the time the lights
changed, the Zumstegs, one or other of them as fast-talking as
both were congenial, had invited Michael to join them and their
daughter Monika for dinner, and he, enchanted by the show of
Californian hospitality, had accepted.

He was instantly smitten with Monika – which, going by pictures of her, is understandable. Her large eyes, set wide apart,
were only a mite less dark than her raven hair, which she wore in a
simple style, brushed back from her high forehead and coaxed
round her ears so as to emphasise the oval shape of her face, the

lint-whiteness of it. She was little more than five feet tall; but even that was pleasing to Michael, who, short himself, tended to feel uncomfortable in the presence of women who loomed over him. Had she been taller – so she told him – she would have taken up modelling. Her small reason for not being a model did not explain why, though she was twenty-five, she had never worked.

Once Michael had let slip what must have seemed to him a couple of disconnected facts – that he was in the middle of divorce preceedings; that his family was extremely rich – Monika appeared to be as captivated by him as he was by her. Two nights after the first, she by then having demurely confessed that she was not a virgin, they took to the same bed.

On her account, he further prolonged his stay in California. He believed that he got to know her well. When he eventually returned to England – there to take up residence in a furnished house, drab of exterior, that the Vestey properties manager had acquired for him on a short-let basis, in Poona Road, in the Kent spa-town, not long ago select, of Royal Tunbridge Wells – his only solace, an inadequate one, at being parted from Monika was his possession of the Harley-Davidson motor-cycle, which he revved without regard for the neighbours and tuned and polished and, once or twice, on days when there was no chance of rain spotting its sparkle, actually rode, attired in a bespoke crash-helmet, a many-pocketed and much-zippered overall of bright blue leather, and glistening black boots, and wearing Reactolite goggles. He fixed a tape-recorder to his telephone so that whenever he rang Monika, which was at least twice a day, she could hear, perhaps better than she heard him, the sound of Tony Bennett singing 'I Left My Heart in San Francisco'. During some of the calls, tongue-tied for words to express his love, he joined in with the lyric of the song; and Monika, who had a sweet voice (had she persevered with music lessons – so she told him – she would have taken up singing as a career), made a trio. It was all very romantic. Before the transatlantic telephone calls had cost the Vestey trust-fund much more than a thousand pounds, Michael asked Monika if she would marry him as soon as his divorce was absolute. Her response was exorbitantly gratifying: she had thought he would never ask, she said, and in the same breath told him that she would board the first available flight to Heathrow, and they would live as man and wife before the event. They cohabited at 12 Poona Road till November

1981, when their union was made proper by a registrar of marriages.

There was nothing subtle about the change that came over Monika. All of a sudden, she became a different woman – or rather, sighing with relief, she threw off the sheep's clothing that she had worn, uncomfortably, in what she considered the good cause of deceiving the easily deceivable Michael. Premaritally, she had relieved her craving for drink covertly, waiting for Michael's elsewhereness before scurrying to a cache of vodka – that drink chosen, not because it was her favourite tipple, but because it left no odour on the breath – and, trusting that Michael would be sympathetic rather than suspicious when she spoke, eyes shyly downcast, of incommoding side-effects throughout her menstrual cycle, pretended that hangovers were headaches brought on by things she would prefer not to talk about. Hangovers apart, the headache-pretence had been useful as an excuse for increasing the number of times when she and Michael, retiring to bed, had gone straight to sleep.

But, directly after the marriage ceremony, she took Michael, who was not a heavy drinker, on a pub-crawl, surprising him as much by her knowledge of the licensed premises of Royal Tunbridge Wells as by the amount she swigged in each of them. And on the wedding night, drunk but not merry, she made no excuse, unless lack of interest can be counted as such, for depriving him of what he had been so looking forward to.

Her breakfast next morning – and on subsequent ones – was slight but unconventional: Benedictine and orange-juice on the rocks. Afterwards, when Michael suggested that they might try out his wedding gift to her of a flashy American car, a white Pontiac Firebird, she told him to fuck off – adding, rather more politely, that she had only asked for a car of her own so that she could get away from him whenever she felt like it, which was most of the time.

Drinking was not Monika's sole vice. Before the marriage, Michael had sometimes wondered how it was that, though he and Monika rarely ate at home, and then only junk-food that he had bought at local take-away places, she always came back for more, considerably more, housekeeping money; and he had been puzzled by the fact that, jumpy and fretful before locking herself in a bathroom, she would emerge looking sleepy but content. Now she removed both quandaries by telling him that she took drugs – preferably cocaine, but heroin if that was all that was on offer. Rather than risk upsetting her by suggesting that she should try to break the habit, he said that she was not to worry her pretty little head about not having enough money to pay for it. According to his subsequent reckoning, the cost was never less than £250 a month. Unless she acquired the drugs from a Harley Street clinic that accepted credit-cards, the payments came from Michael's monthly stipend of £1250. On one occasion, having bought more cocaine than was usual, she cashed a cheque for £700 that he had given her to settle a long-overdue demand for rates.

Monika's alcoholism and drug-reliance were, between them, less depressing to Michael than another secret that came to light – this time accidentally – after no more than a week or so of their married life. This was that she was bi-sexual. A house two doors away – more gaily painted than theirs, in blue and white – was the home of a young solicitor, his wife Rosemary, and their three children. Rosemary, it subsequently transpired, was one of a number of married women who, unattracted to membership of the Royal Tunbridge Wells branch of the Mothers' Union or the Townswomen's Guild, had formed a fairly secret society, known as Us Girls, for the purpose of having a sort of 'naughty fun' among themselves that, by its nature, was preclusive of contributions from the husbands; the high-spot of the Us Girls year was a fortnight of frolicking on the Aegean island of Mikonos, south-west of the island of Lesbos. One evening, Michael returned home earlier than Monika had expected him, and found her and Rosemary, both in a state of undress, canoodling on the living-room carpet. According to the account of the incident given by Rosemary to another of Us Girls: 'He seemed to meekly accept what was happening and, far from being outraged, suggested we use the double-bed upstairs while he slept that night in the attic.' A clue as to whether or not the suggestion was accepted probably reposes in a diary that Rosemary was keeping, intending to use some of her entries as the basis of episodes in a pornographic novel that she was writing: an art-fashioned-from-nature enterprise that she firmly believed would do for Royal Tunbridge Wells what *Peyton Place* had done for Manchester, New Hampshire. In breaks between the gymnastic activities at closed meetings of Us Girls, Rosemary gave readings from her diary, and during one such literary interlude, weeks after Michael's discovery of her and his wife on the Axminster, she sent a buzz round the assembled company by revealing that she was still 'having if off' with Monika – *at Michael's request*: 'He actually encouraged the affair because he knew it made Monika happy. If she was happy, she would stay with him.'

Michael's fear that he would lose Monika was premature. She told Rosemary that she was determined to remain his wife for exactly two years – 'and then force a divorce, screwing the Vesteys for at least fifty grand'. She said much the same to Michael's first wife, Alison, whom she visited in Maidencombe without his knowledge. (She had forbidden him to see Alison or his son; but, disobeying her for once, he arranged clandestine meetings with them in a car-park in Bristol.) I cannot tell when, or why, she went to see Alison. The fact that she had already trained the pet cockatoo that accompanied her to say 'Piss off, Michael' indicates that the visit took place no earlier than the spring of 1982. Apart from the bird's oft-spoken, though in the circumstances irrelevant, remark, and Monika's comment regarding her intention to stay with Michael in aid of lavish severance pay, Alison remembers only that her surprise-visitor, declining an offer of tea, took pills that one may surmise were not aspirin, swilling them down with neat gin, and chain-smoked cigarettes of cannabis that she rolled herself.

In July, Monika and Rosemary went off on holiday to Innsbruck. Rosemary, a keen photographer, took lots of indoor snaps, none of which she could have asked Boots the Chemist to develop. She had thought to include in her luggage her youngest child's rubber duck; and while Monika, lying in the bath, did things with the duck that its manufacturer had never envisaged, Rosemary excitedly and insatiably clicked her Instamatic. (Perhaps because Monika so treasured the memory of her lover's pleasure from these photographic sessions, some months later she bought herself a real duck, which she called Daffy.) Halfway through the Austrian holiday, Monika telephoned Michael, not, of course, to say that she wished he was there, but to tell him to send her money. Over-obligingly, he took it to her. Arriving at the hotel at a time when most of the guests were up and about, he found that Monika and Rosemary were not. His interruption of whatever they were doing put both of them in a bad mood: he afterwards said that Rosemary was 'very bitchy'; Monika used words similar to those that she had taught her cockatoo to say. Leaving the money on the dressing table, he departed.

It may be that that experience caused him to ask the Vestey properties manager to find him a home well away from Royal Tunbridge Wells: well away from Rosemary and the rest of the Us Girls gang. In any event, in August he and Monika moved to Lambourne House, an expensive conversion of adjoining farm-buildings in the Buckinghamshire village of Bledlow Ridge, five miles north-west of High Wycombe, and fifteen from the western outskirts of London.

Monika wasted no time in finding replacements for Rosemary. On her very first trip to High Wycombe, she made the acquaintance of a lesbian waitress in a pizza parlour, a girl called Karen, with whom she had sex before returning home; by the end of the week, she was on intimate terms not only with Karen, but with most of Karen's many women-friends. Though, in the months that foll-owed, hardly a day passed when she did not drive to High Wycombe, first to eat an excess of pizza, then to keep an appointment, tête-à-tête, with one or other or several of the local lesbians, she still had the energy to seek to verify the boast of sexual versatility that she made to a casual visitor to Lambourne House: 'I can fuck any man, any woman, better than anybody else can. I'm AC/DC. I go with anybody.'

One man with whom she planned to go was a guest at a party that she and Michael attended. But Michael, emboldened by booze, put his foot down: literally. When, at the end of the party, she refused to get into his custom-built Mini, he drove full-tilt at the prospective adulterer's car, severely damaging both vehicles. Not content with volunteering a statement to the police to the effect that her husband – 'who should be locked away in an asylum' – had attempted to cause grievous bodily harm to the other man (who, as he stated, was nowhere near his car when it was rammed), Monika informed the police that Michael was in illegal possession of firearms that he had bought in America: resultantly, Lambourne House was searched, the weapons confiscated, and Michael fined £6000. All of that was so upsetting to Michael that he had to receive tranquillising treatment at a hospital. Monika, accompanying him on his first visit, made a poor impression on the doctor, who described her in his notes as 'a vociferous and obnoxious American who was drunk and swigging whisky from a flask during the interview'.

Had Michael been as vindictive as his wife, he would have directed the attention of the police search-team to the herb-garden, where Monika was trying to grow marijuana; or to her handbag, in which she kept a pearl-handled .22 automatic pistol. She had shown that weapon – and other esoteric contents of her bag, including a vaginal vibrator – to Cheryl Richardson, a middle-aged resident of a nearby council estate who, since her husband, a welder by trade, was unemployed, had agreed to do some of the Tellings' housework. The Richardsons had come to know their wealthy neighbours through Citizens-Band radio, which had been their consuming hobby for some time and which was Michael's latest mechanical craze, his on-air codename being 'Police Inspector'.

Separately or together, the Richardsons were the most frequent visitors to Lambourne House. Presumably Mr Richardson was absent when Monika informed Cheryl that 'if she screwed her, she would never want another man'. Mr Richardson was left with a number of striking memories of the Tellings' domestic life:

'Once when my wife and I went round, Monika asked us if we would like coffee. I expected her to get it, but she turned round and said to Michael: "Get off your fucking arse, you mother-fucker, and make them a coffee." He kissed her hands and the top of her head, but she kept on and on. I wanted to take him to the garden and knock some sense into him and tell him not to take it. He was very much frightened of her. She had threatened him that if he ever hurt her, her father and brothers would come over and sort him out. Once when they were play-wrestling in the kitchen, she kneed him in the private parts. He went very white but did nothing.'

In February 1983, Michael came to the conclusion – or thought he did – that he and Monika were incompatible. Having told her that he was going away 'to consider the future', he flew to Australia, and there discussed his marital problems with his stepfather. But he couldn't resist telephoning Monika each day. Perhaps because of the time-difference, she was usually in bed when the calls came through. As he had fixed a two-way amplifier to the bedside telephone, she was able to continue whatever she was doing with whoever was in bed with her while carrying on a conversation with him: sometimes the bed-sharer was a lesbian student of sociology who planned to become a counsellor of delinquent girls, sometimes a painter and decorator, and on one occasion she was sandwiched between a sales representative and his fiancée. (The travelling man subsequently stated: 'There was nothing improper about the situation. It was the only bed in the house.')

Michael returned to England in mid-March. Undeterred by the heavy fine that he – or rather, the administrators of the Vestey trust-fund – had had to pay because of his illegal possession of firearms, he brought back with him a Marlin .303 rifle and ammunition for it. Monika was in bed with the aforementioned painter and decorator when he telephoned her from the Hyde Park Hotel, begging her to come to him there 'for a second honeymoon'. Relieved by the call – for there were still eight months to go until their wedding anniversary, when she could leave him wealthily – she hurriedly dressed, telling her artisan-companion to do likewise, and drove to the hotel. Michael gave her what he called 'a making-up present', a diamond necklace, and she let him make love to her for the first time since their move from Royal Tunbridge Wells.

They returned to Bledlow Ridge on Monday, 28 March, the day before Michael was due to enter the hospital for a check on his mental condition.

Next morning, a sunny one, Monika told him to hurry up and leave. She wanted to get on with her own life, she said.

He went to the bedroom. Monika assumed that he was packing an overnight bag. But when he re-entered the living room, he was carrying the Marlin rifle. He leant it against the wall.

As Monika came towards him, he picked up the rifle, levelled it at her, and fired. She fell between the flower-patterned sofas on either side of the fireplace. He cocked the rifle and shot her again. And again. Two of the bullets entered her chest, and the third pierced her throat.

He stood for a while, simply staring into space, and then, weeping, told the corpse that he was very sorry for what he had done and asked its forgiveness. Meanwhile, the cockatoo, fussed by the explosions, squawked monotonously: 'Piss off, Michael.'

Some time afterwards, he made two telephone calls: one to the hospital, to cancel his appointment, and the other to Cheryl Richardson, telling her not to come to the house till he invited her. He also dragged the body into a spare room, lifted it on to a camp-bed and draped a sheet over it, not so as to cover the face, which he kissed repeatedly.

During the following few days, he spent much time in the spare room, caressing the body, kissing the face, and talking as if Monika were alive. He wished that the Vesteys had granted him a house with its own chapel, so that he could have given Monika consecrated rest. *Rigor mortis* had gone by Sunday, and in the morning, about the time when the bells of the village church were ringing for matins, he moved the body to an out-house which, months before, he had started to turn into a sauna-bath but left uncompleted because of Monika's insistence on having an open-air Jacuzzi whirlpool. Ingeniously, he propped the body upright. He did not bother to put a lock on the door. Later, however, he installed an electric air-freshener.

Straightway after employing an odd-job man to shampoo the carpets in the house, he called up Mrs Richardson and, saying that Monika had left him, asked her to become his daily-woman, doing the shopping and preparing meals as well as keeping the place spick and span. She proved to be a treasure, not least by staying late on evenings when he was feeling specially lonely. He had always loved dogs, but Monika had refused to let him have one of his own; now he bought two Alsatian puppies, and delighted in them.

Within ten days of Monika's death, he started using his CB-radio equipment again, preferring the codename of 'Snake' to that of 'Police Inspector'. You will recall that he had got to know the Richardsons through CB radio. By an odd coincidence, he, as 'Snake', linked up, if that is the expression, with a woman calling herself 'Chanel' who lived on the same small council estate as the Richardsons. Her husband had deserted her and their two children, and so she was eager for male companionship. Following a short exchange of CB jargon, she and Michael met for dinner at a Chinese restaurant in High Wycombe; afterwards, they repaired to Lambourne House, where they continued talking – chiefly about their curtailed marriages – until sunrise. Later that day, having seen to her children, Chanel returned. The relationship lasted for a month, during which time none of Michael's attempts at intercourse was successful; perhaps he was inhibited by mental pictures of what was propped up in the out-house. It seemed to Chanel that 'Monika was always on his mind':

'He even compared my fingernails with hers. He said that hers were extremely long, and that she had attacked him with them. He said that she was not very nice to him – basically, he was glad she was gone. On 16 April he arrived at my home with a half-length silver-fox coat which he offered to me. He said he had bought it for Monika, but she had thrown it back at him. He bought me presents – a new CB radio and scent and bath-oil from Paris – and he offered to buy me clothes. I think he was trying to buy love and affection. He told me he was a member of the SAS, and indicated that he had been suspended for doing something wrong. He didn't say where he had been with the SAS, but indicated it might have been the Falklands, although I didn't believe him.'

Chanel was not the only female CB enthusiast to have an affair with Michael during the spring and hot summer of the year: his favourite among the others seems to have been a woman who, though possessing no medical qualification, went by the name of 'Night Nurse'. Additionally, a divorcée from the nearby village of Downley who had been a close friend of Monika's slept with him at odd times of the day – never the night – throughout June and July.

Towards the end of August, he received a most unwelcome communication from the Vestey properties manager, suggesting that he should plan a vacation, since arrangements were being made for extensive refurbishment of Lambourne House. This so preyed on his mind that, while driving Mrs Richardson back from a freezer centre in High Wycombe, he blurted out to her that he had killed Monika. She thought that he had 'flipped his lid', and scolded him for making a distasteful joke like that. 'He said it was true – that the body was stinking in the sauna. I just didn't believe it.' One wonders how she managed to change the subject.

Next day or the day after, he hired a self-drive van, in lieu of a hearse, and having placed Monika's body, much lighter by now, in the back of it, together with a cleaver and a polythene bag, drove to the West Country –towards, but not quite as far as, Maidencombe. Night had fallen by the time he parked on the hard shoulder of the A38 at Haldon Hill, overlooking the Devon and Exeter Racecourse. Waiting till he could see no headlights in either direction, he slid the body from the van and dragged it up an incline, through gorse and bracken, to a small clearing skirted by conifers. Once he had got his breath back, he hacked off the head. The fact that he had not thought to bring a torch may explain why one of the blows from the cleaver went so wide of the mark that several teeth were dislodged, to fall among the fir-needles and cones. Carefully, perhaps reverently, he slipped the head into the polythene bag, positioned the body in a sitting position against a tree, and, carrying the cleaver in one hand, the bag in the other, returned to the van, the doors of which he had left wide, hoping that the soft breeze curling over the brow of the hill would carry away the noisome small. He drove back to Lambourne House, and, not knowing where else to put it, stowed Monika's head, still wrapped, in the boot of his Mini, which was parked in the garage. Having rested, he bought a can of live maggots from an anglers' suppliers in Marlow and spilt them into the bag.

On Saturday, 3 September, a motorist, fit to burst, parked on Haldon Hill and ran up the incline and into the clearing – but, unrelieved, scuttled back to his car and drove on till he came to a police station, where, retching as he spoke, he told of his observation of a headless corpse.

The discovery was reported in the Sunday papers. Reports in Monday's noted that the remains were those of a short woman, probably in her twenties, naturally dark (though, of course, the hair on the absent head may have been dyed), and that the upper part of the torso was clad in a white T-shirt with the words 'Souvenir du Maroc' making it seem a valuable clue towards identification, the lower part in 'fun shorts' of salmon-pink silk. That evening, the discovery was mentioned in a news programme on television that was watched, at Lambourne House, by Michael and Mrs Richardson. He lurched out of the room. 'I could hear him vomiting in the bathroom,' Cheryl subsequently recalled 'I didn't pay too much attention because he is a diabetic, and if he doesn't eat, he gets sick.'

But by Thursday she had, against her will, connected the incident with what Michael had said to her on the way back from the freezer centre. She and her husband went to the police. Among other things she told them was that Monika, shortly before her disappearance, had undergone surgery for a gum disorder. The teeth found in the clearing were shown to the dental surgeon, who identified them as his late patient's.

Michael was pleased to be arrested. He talked to policemen about his life with Monika, his life afterwards, for six hours, for much of that time sitting cross-legged on the floor in the corner of an interview room, and later reminisced to other interested parties. His main concern was that his two Alsatians should be cared for.

'I had a hundred and one reasons for killing Monika,' he said, 'and I just snapped in the end. I don't just mean nagging – she was horrible in most ways. But it didn't justify killing. What can justify killing? She openly told me she slept with other men and also that she was a lesbian. She often taunted me with these affairs and constantly belittled my sexual efforts, saying I was only good for money. From the day we married, she changed in her attitude towards me and became very aggressive and different. She could switch on and off like a light. I was very confused in my mind at the time I shot her, and I had no clear idea why I did it. Even when I finally disposed of her body, I could not bear to be apart from her, and on impulse decapitated her.' The only time he displayed anger was when one of the interrogators suggested that he had cut a wire-fence between the road and the clearing. 'I would never do a thing like that,' he exclaimed. 'I'm not a vandal. I don't despoil the countryside.'

He stood trial at Exeter Crown Court in June 1984. The Vesteys had hired the worthily-expensive Queen's Counsel, George Carman, to support his plea that he was not guilty of murder but of manslaughter, by reason of diminished responsibility. As is disgracefully usual in such cases, the testimony of the psychiatrist on the side of the Crown was diametrically different from that of the psychiatrist enlisted by the defence. Mr Carman called a representative sample of lesbians who had enjoyed liaisons with Monika (Rosemary, the wife of a solicitor, was not among the chosen) and one or two of the Buckinghamshire Female Citizens Band. The trial, which was allowed to drag on for nine days, resulted in the verdict for which Michael had pleaded, and the judge sentenced him to a term of life imprisonment, without expressing a view as to the meaning of life.

When confessing to the police, Michael had said: 'I suppose I'll be in prison thirty, forty, fifty years.' One hopes, not just for his irresponsible sake, that any efforts financed by his family to make the supposition ludicrous will prove unsuccessful; and that none of the money spent by the Vesteys in aid of his release will be deemed tax-deductible by the Inland Revenue.

Beard
ON
ENTERTAINING

'He was an innovator, an experimenter, a missionary in bringing the gospel of good cooking to the home table' Craig Claiborne

---

James Beard's classic cookbook demonstrates how to achieve simple elegance on every occasion from breakfast for four to buffets for forty. Including more than one hundred marvellous menus, with over six hundred delicious and imaginative recipes, *and* a comprehensive wine guide, this delightful compendium comes from the acknowledged master of American cookery, who has influenced food writers from Julia Child to Madhur Jaffrey.

NON-FICTION   0-7472-3056-0   £7.95

MALEE

—

TIGER CLAW AND VELVET PAW

—

The erotic odyssey of Thai prostitute

The world of Suzie Wong . . .

The daughter of a Thai rice farmer, Malee is forced to leave her village and enter domestic service at the age of fourteen. Raped by her master, she flees to the nearest open door – the local brothel.

Realising that prostitution offers her only chance of survival, Malee becomes a showdancing star, devising erotic spectacles of Oriental sensuality.

She moves on from the world of the American GI to the cosmopolitan life of Bangkok and finally settles in the red light district of Hamburg.

Explicit and touchingly honest, Malee's story explores a sexual underworld of fantasy and compulsion exploited by whore and punter alike.

NON-FICTION   0-7472-3047-1   £2.50

Headline books are available at your bookshop or newsagent, or can be ordered from the following address:

Headline Book Publishing PLC
Cash Sales Department
PO Box 11
Falmouth
Cornwall
TR10 9EN
England

UK customers please send cheque or postal order (no currency), allowing 60p for postage and packing for the first book, plus 25p for the second book and 15p for each additional book ordered up to a maximum charge of £1.90 in UK.

BFPO customers please allow 60p for postage and packing for the first book, plus 25p for the second book and 15p per copy for the next seven books, thereafter 9p per book.

Overseas and Eire customers please allow £1.25 for postage and packing for the first book, plus 75p for the second book and 28p for each subsequent book.